TEAR DOWN THE IRON CURTAINS

Books in the "Fighting Hatred with Writing" Series

❖ *The Return of al-Qaeda: When a Dreaded Terrorist Reaches the Turning Point*
❖ *Tear Down the Iron Curtains: A Letter to the KKK*

Tear Down the Iron Curtains

Curtains

—A Letter to the KKK

Dele Ajaja

iUniverse, Inc.

New York Lincoln Shanghai

Tear Down the Iron Curtains
—A Letter to the KKK

iUniverse books may be ordered through booksellers or by contacting:

iUniverse
2021 Pine Lake Road, Suite 100
Lincoln, NE 68512
www.iuniverse.com
1-800-Authors (1-800-288-4677)

Because of the dynamic nature of the Internet, any Web addresses or links contained in this book may have changed since publication and may no longer be valid.

The views expressed in this work are solely those of the author and do not necessarily reflect the views of the publisher, and the publisher hereby disclaims any responsibility for them.

ISBN: 978-0-595-47082-2 (pbk)
ISBN: 978-0-595-91364-0 (ebk)

Printed in the United States of America

TRIBUTE

❖To the victims of hatred worldwide, fair-minded people
share your pains everywhere

❖To peace-loving youths around the world, you are the hope of tomorrow
and the trustees of a peaceful future

❖To all who resist hatred, the silent workers who cement a fractured world, you are
the sweeteners. Without you, the world would be a bitter place

- *INSIDE* -

▼

PRÉCIS

Do you expect an upheaval when a black man writes the Ku Klux Klan? Think again. There is an alternative to hatred. *Tear Down the Iron Curtains* is a unique and necessary attempt to reconcile races, cultures, faiths, and other groups. Mankind began the twenty-first century with unprecedented cultural, religious, and gang tensions. Suspicion among peoples with diverse ways of life has risen to an all-time high during the past decade. Terrorism is now a borderless phenomenon that haunts every nation. Expressed and unexpressed bitterness among nations is making pessimists out of those who thought the world would no longer witness major conflicts. The menace of gangs is not leaving our cities, and formerly non-violent neighborhoods are becoming restless.

Should the peace-loving majority of the people around the world submit to these undesirable trends? It is not a clever choice to leave a bitterly divided world to the coming generations. More than ever, the conscientious among us, regardless of their races, colors, and religions, need to come together and speak up against intolerance. The world will lose its body, spirit, and soul to evil if fine men, women, and children keep mute when it matters. The outstanding *Letter to the KKK* is a deliberate effort to reconcile the diverse peoples everywhere. Mankind has no healthier option than fashioning a mutually supportive civilization that curtails the intolerance of man by man. *Tear Down the Iron Curtains*, a blend of diversity, nonviolence, social justice, and anti-gang themes, has something for everyone, including youths, adults, institutions, and groups that oppose any form of hatred. Dele Ajaja engages his personal experiences to advocate tolerance.

HONOR ROLL

Not only did these people talk, they used their influence to advance human causes. Thank you for holding the world together this far!

❖ The Unknown Peacemaker is any man, woman, or child who fosters unity and understanding among individuals, groups, and cultures. This is you, the reader.

❖ Mother Teresa, the 1979 Nobel Peace Prize winner, lived and died among the poor in Calcutta, India.

❖ Lady Diana, the late Princess of Wales, who her admirers fondly called the Princess of Hearts, gave her heart to the downtrodden everywhere.

❖ Rosa Louise Parks, the mother of the modern-day civil rights movement, refused to give up her seat on a bus, leading to the Montgomery Bus Boycott of 1955.

❖ Mahatma Gandhi was the modest, nonviolent activist and founding father of modern India. His peaceful engagements influenced others around the world.

❖ Kwame Nkrumah, the father of modern Ghana and African nationalist, set the agenda for the liberation of Africa from colonialists.

❖ Martin Luther King Jr., the 1964 Nobel Peace Prize winner and icon of American civil rights activism, sought dignity and equality for all races.

❖ Anwar Sadat, the late Egyptian head of state who shared the 1978 Nobel Peace Prize with Israeli Prime Minister Menachem Begin, tried to unite Arabs and Jews.

❖ Cesar Estrada Chavez was a civil rights activist and labor leader. His actions led the struggle to procure better treatment for migrant workers in the United States.

❖ Tai Solarin, foremost teacher and social justice advocate, lived and died advocating for a socially responsible Africa.

❖ Pope John Paul II, the soldier of faith, fought to the very end for understanding among religions and cultures.

❖ Nelson Mandela, the conscience of Africa who shared the 1993 Nobel Peace Prize with Prime Minister Frederik de Klerk, ended apartheid in a divided South Africa.

❖ President Jimmy Carter, the 2002 Nobel Peace Prize winner, is a universal statesman.

❖ Desmond Tutu, the 1984 Nobel Peace Prize winner, helped to resolve the problems of apartheid in South Africa.

❖ The Dalai Lama, the nonviolent spiritual leader of Tibetan Buddhism, was the 1998 Nobel Peace Prize winner.

❖ Kofi Annan, former United Nations Secretary-General, stood against hostilities between groups and nations.

❖ President Bill Clinton, an advocate for social change with a big heart for mankind, made the world his constituency.

❖ Jesse Jackson, American civil rights and social justice advocate, dedicated his life to equal rights and justice for all.

❖ Bill Moyer, the renowned nonviolent American social change activist, spoke on behalf of the weak.

❖ Bill Gates is one of the few wealthy and conscientious men who understand the essence of riches.

❖ Al Sharpton, civil rights activist, social justice advocate, actor, and preacher, keeps the ideals alive.

❖ Vice President Al Gore, the 2007 Nobel Peace Prize winner, leads the strenuous campaign against global pollution.

❖ Oprah Winfrey, the talk show host who goes beyond talking, redeems lives with her resources.

❖ Paul David Hewson (Bono), the lead singer of U2 and social change advocate, gives his all to the downtrodden.

❖ Robert Frederick Zenon (Bob) Geldof, Irish singer, songwriter, and social justice activist, leads a heartfelt campaign against poverty in the world.

❖ Gani Fawehinmi (Senior Advocate of Nigeria), the people's lawyer and prisoner of conscience, dedicated his life to a Nigeria devoid of bad governance.

❖ Daw Aung San Suu Kyi, the 1991 Nobel Peace Prize winner, is the Myanmar nonviolent prisoner of conscience.

❖ Abubakar Dangiwa Umar, an outstanding, retired Nigerian soldier, is a model of what a soldier should be and a statesman extraordinaire.

❖ Southern Poverty Law Center, the Montgomery, Alabama, nonprofit organization, fights hatred and promotes civil rights.

❖ Doctors Without Borders/Médecins Sans Frontières, the secular and nonprofit medical organization, cares for the challenged regions of the world.

PROLOGUE

▼

Cowardice asks the question, 'Is it safe?' Expediency asks the question, 'Is it politic?'
But conscience asks the question, 'Is it right?' And there comes a time when one must
take a position that is neither safe, nor politic, nor popular but because conscience tells
one it is right.
—Martin Luther King Jr.

Moments after I witnessed a racially motivated conflict along a street in Accra, the capital of Ghana, I said reflexively, "I have a mission." I was taking an evening walk, years ago, when a car knocked down a pedestrian. The driver was white; the pedestrian was black. Apparently, that was the only evidence a few rascals needed to color the accident as a racially provoked attempt by the driver to hurt a member of the group. It was an unusual scene because the people of Ghana are very pleasant. They love foreigners and treat them with respect. It is un-African to treat foreigners shabbily. The continent maintains its long history of hospitality toward visitors. Hence, the few dissenters seemed to be simply looking for trouble.

"*You wan' kill my brother because he be black?*" asked a muscular male in broken English. "*Slave trade time don pass,*" he added as some Good Samaritans aided the slightly bruised pedestrian.

Justifiably, many Africans were outraged by the transatlantic slave trade that ravaged the continent a couple of centuries ago, but the overwhelming majority of the people were forbearing and hoping for a better future instead. It was unusual for people to provoke trouble in the street on the basis of that bitter part of history.

"*We go show them say slave trade don pass!*" bellowed the firebrand leader of the group.

The daring set I was about to confront intimidated me, but I chose to stand by the facts anyway. Evidently, the visibly worried driver did not knock down the pedestrian purposefully. I understood the feelings of the men who were unhappy with the past, like I was, but the overwhelming majority of Africans would not carry lights and search for a fight on that basis. Africans were aware that a well-defined wronged party would not remain if they retaliated against the inhumane and exploitative slave trade indiscreetly. We cannot bury the history, but we should never allow the resulting anger to create further problems for the coming generations of mankind.

"Color has nothing to do with this!" I yelled.

I could feel the sweat forming on my forehead while I tried to slow my quickened breath. The thumping of my heart did not make things easy as I struggled to counter the scary troublemakers, but I acted somehow. I had always believed that a hard-hitting ailment required a matching panacea. I realized that talking softly to the group would not ease their tone. It was certainly one of those times when I had to make radical decisions. I knew the irate hoodlums might try to attack me. I had to do something unconventional as the driver and I faced the unpredictable pack.

"I will ensure that all of you go to jail if you do anything to the driver," I said, dipping a hand inside my pocket and bringing out the little recorder that I carried with me most of the time.

I had always believed that reporters should carry recorders around. When a story broke, it did not wait for people. I clicked something on the recorder and pretended it was a walkie-talkie.

"Yeah! Police Commander Boateng …" I started talking to an imaginary police officer.

I became more courageous as I reassured myself that I was in charge of the event. I looked at the ringleader intently. I was apparently getting his attention. The man, who was very bold a moment ago, started toning down his menacing impression. His hard glare melted into an attentive gaze. I knew my act had impacted him. I felt the boldness storming out of me as the troublemaker backed away gradually.

"*You dey support Obroni against your black brothers?*" suggested the man tenderly.

"The fact that I stopped my brothers from doing wrong indicates I would stop anyone from doing wrong," I corrected the erroneous impression made by the man.

"*He be secret policeman*," whispered the ringleader. He and his lieutenants then withdrew.

The startled driver's face showed relief. He was amazed that I stood up for the facts, even when the wrongdoers and I shared a skin color. "Tackle prejudice, regardless of the color of the people involved," I advised.

"I'm a part of the solution, not a part of the problem," I reaffirmed to myself on the way home.

That night, I had difficulty falling asleep as I questioned why the world remained in a state of distrust despite years of civilization. The myriad of racial disagreements around the world concerned me. I had many questions, but I only had a few answers. Why do humans loathe one another? Who will save us from ourselves? Why do people lump others together in judgment? When will humans start treating humans with respect? How are we going to get the message that the world is wide enough for all of us to coexist happily? Can't we all just get along? More questions continued.

The following morning, I woke up with further questions that yearned for answers. I could not think of a cure-all for the global ailment. I knew I might not be able to stop those who chose to hate, but I could be vocal in peacemaking. A few weeks later, I started a nonprofit organization, Global Love Project, to nurture understanding among peoples and groups. I requested willing newspaper editors to donate spaces for weekly snippets to educate people about diversity and tolerance. A mission had begun.

Tear Down the Iron Curtains is about minimizing distrust between races and creating mutual respect among faiths, cultures, and other groups. Intolerance remains one of the disconcerting realities of our time that many prefer to ignore or treat as the norm. Ignoring prejudice is certainly not shrewd. It will cause us to bequeath a bitterly divided world to our offspring.

It is the responsibility of everyone with a heart to start building bridges and smoothing sharp edges between cultures and groups. This is an arduous task, but the conscientious individuals among us owe posterity the debt of remaking the world. We could only shirk this obligation to the peril of our children and the generations after them. God bless the world.

CHAPTER 1

▼

GROUND ZERO

Where there is hatred, let me sow love. Where there is injury, pardon. Where there is doubt, faith.
—St. Francis of Assisi

Dear KKK,

I woke up this morning thinking about our brothers and sisters who passed away on September 11, 2001. I regretted we could not say good-bye or declare how much we loved them before they departed to the great beyond. That's why I decided to state the importance of love in a fractured world. Absence of love motivated the reprehensible acts of terrorism against our nation and humanity. Raging with hatred for fellow humans, the adversaries gave their lives so others might die. I have pondered why man hates and offers a free rein to *viocracy*, that is, violence of the people, by the people, and for the people. I have tasked myself to find the answer why humans remain vindictive decades after denouncing the Holocaust. I should know that mankind has yet to comprehend the uncomplicated logic behind diversity. But man has made the complicated journey to the moon. His influences have reached farther heavenly bodies. Amazing!

KKK, do you wonder what part of getting along is difficult for man to understand? Getting along was supposed to be a universal gesture that was understood in every land and clime. We live in a world where laughing, smiling, and nodding are understood universally. We dwell on a planet where crying, sighing, and handshaking are implicit everywhere. Why should getting along be different? Why must respecting one another be a thorny gesture to comprehend? Why should it be tricky for mankind to appreciate a universal idea that touches our very existence? I had the premonition that the coming generations would find present generations weird because it was difficult for us to get along. They may wonder why their ancestors failed to decipher an appealing gesture when we did not live in a world where smiling meant one thing in one culture and something else in another. Our progeny may wonder why we appreciated arts, sciences, and technologies but failed to behold the splendor of diversity.

Surprisingly, it took the ugly adversity of 9/11 to remind us about the beauty of diversity. The enemy's actions, which were meant to shatter the body, soul, and spirit of our nation, united us instead. A person's race no longer matters. Brotherhood became fashionable. KKK, do you recall how we hugged and sighed in the street, seeking solace in each other's arms in the wake of the American tragedy? No man feared the other man's skin would glue to his as we embraced. From Manhattan to Jersey City across the great Hudson River, Brooklyn to Staten Island, the Bronx to Ellis Island, Queens to Long Island, or Arlington to Shanksville, race did not count anywhere in America.

People no longer believed the adage, "God for us all and every man for himself." Strangers helped strangers without thinking about skin color. Whites opened their doors for blacks. Blacks lent a hand to injured whites. Hispanics assisted exhausted Asians to their feet. Asians wiped off the dust from weary Hispanic faces. Jews pulled hurt Native Americans to safety. Native Americans gave water to thirsty Jews. Middle Easterners comforted the people of the Caribbean. The people of the Caribbean consoled the Middle Easterners. Christians did not ask if the strangers they hauled from the fiery rubble downtown Manhattan were Muslims. Muslims did not refuse to assist Catholics. Catholics did not check if those they lifted were Hindu. Hindus supported Protestants instinctively. Protestants did not despise atheists before offering support. Lutherans did not sneer at Buddhists. Buddhists did not mind hugging Jewish rabbis. On that day, Kabbalah practitioners, Shintoists, Baha'i devotees, Sikhs, Scientologists, Taoists, and Zoroastrians were not any different than Unitarians. Compassion was the only religion that mankind recognized on that day. Bias, intolerance, prejudice, and stereotyping were out of town. It was a matter of men, women, boys, and girls claiming their memberships of the human race, regardless of their nationalities, skin colors, religions, affiliations, or gangs. No one insisted on being black, white, Native American, Hispanic, Asian, Alaskan, or Pacific Islander. At Ground Zero, people were simply helping people. No one called anyone names. There were no petty-minded racists. There were only fellow humans, searching for relief in others' arms. That was the day that the *Bloods* and *Crips* discarded their colors and became brothers. That was the day that providence revealed the beauty that lived in ugly.

It was such a paradox that tragedy brought out the best in man. KKK, can you believe that we relapsed into the old way soon after the frenzy of togetherness?

"Humans have short memories," you probably thought just now.

"To thy diverse racial tents, O brothers!" we said, gesturing to each other as we withdrew into our assorted groups once again.

How incredible! Man will become humble and embrace others when tragedy strikes and the fear of the unknown manifests. But he will ditch brothers and fellow compatriots when he feels better. Why do we act like brothers only when it is convenient? Why do we become unwilling acquaintances only when we can handle our own?

KKK, the enemies did not draw boundaries between us when they struck. Skin colors, religions, classes, and gangs meant nothing to the extremists. The bigots labeled us as a bunch of tainted and faithless people who deserved to die together with disgrace. They included black, white, Christian, Muslim, Jew, Buddhist, Hindu, agnostic, male, female, young, old, rich, poor, upright, and perverted people in this group. They drew no lines between peoples.

Those who encouraged the acts of terrorism against our land disregarded the faith they professed and misrepresented God. They affronted millions of faithful and nonviolent Muslims across the globe. If they had thought about faith and God constructively, they would have understood that an overwhelming majority of Muslims abhorred the shedding of innocent blood and that God was not a fanatical assassin. The mass murderers, those rampaging bulls in mankind's china shop, ravenous vultures among human chicks, and famished wolves among man's sheep, hated us all. The illegitimate offspring of circumstance that imposed themselves on God, faith, and cultures regarded no race. The blighted sons of destruction that hid behind faith, cultures, and groups to harm innocent children, defenseless women, and frail elderly people cared less about God.

KKK, you and I should not partake in the burden of haters. Sorrow is their legacy. Tears are their bequest. Sweat is their inheritance. Confusion is their heritage. Disarray is their birthright. I saw two columns of light at Ground Zero, connecting the earth to heaven. In unison, they challenged the haters that hurt, maimed, and killed the innocent. Haters' souls have questions to answer in the morning. The day confronts their spirits. The night tackles their bodies. Their consciences are grilled around the clock. I could feel the intimidated souls of the bigots bowing before the bold souls of the innocent. Forever would the gentle spirits of the innocent make haters' spirits uncomfortable! Haters, the cold, callous, and condemned brood of malevolence, will have no place to rest forever.

Pardon my frankness! There is no better way to hail evil. The vile agents of polarization deserve no kind words. Everything about haters remains conflicting. They embrace wickedness even when informed minds acknowledge that wickedness opposes goodness. Haters understand good from evil, but they prefer evil. On the contrary, the worst among haters recognize the pleasure and camaraderie in unity among men. They address their kinds as "brothers," but they regard other humans as adversaries. They know there is strength in brotherhood, but they prefer divisions among men. Haters are diabolical, divisive, manipulative, narrow-minded, selfish, degraded, mean, perverted, faithless, and short of goodwill for others. KKK, no one should seek after the inheritance of haters. The depravity that comes with the minds that hate should not become our portion.

Haters are truly myopic for limiting brotherhood to their own. It takes broad-minded people to foresee how pleasant and orderly it would be for the whole of mankind to live in brotherhood. It takes rational minds with vision and mission to envision a functional world for all, including diverse peoples, religious, atheist, men, women, boys, girls, affluent, and underprivileged. It takes profound minds to reason profoundly. It takes lucid minds to ration justice rationally. Warped minds uphold brotherhood for their like, but they lack the audacity to share goodwill with all. They fume with ego and lack respect for fellow men. Deplorably, the blinkered, ignorant, and bigots assume they know all things because they know some of the things under their noses. Regrettably, they know nothing about things beyond their noses. They are so indolent that they do not understand or appreciate others.

KKK, I consider it an affront on mankind when we come together as brothers at Ground Zero, but resort to calling each other names soon after. Who is fooling whom when we stand together and respect each other in the face of a tragedy, but brandish egos when dread wanes? Do you flourish by fooling me? Or do I thrive by deceiving you? What do we earn from hoodwinking each other? Double whamming is our lot when we con one another, KKK. What would it profit your children if you fool me? What would it benefit my kids if I swindle you? The rest of the world would laugh at us if we came together when it hurts, but play hide-and-seek with each other when relief comes our way. We gamble, gabble, and jumble away our children's tomorrow when we ignore bias, prejudice, stereotype, discrimination, bigotry, gangs, and social injustices.

KKK, I was not a lone voice in the wilderness when I asked mankind to be truthful to himself. You would recall how Polonius advised his son Laertes in Shakespeare's *Hamlet*:

> "This above all: to thine own self be true,
> And it must follow, as the night the day,
> Thou canst not then be false to any man."

We are the world; the single body that must be true to itself.

I have an idea, KKK. Let's hate hatred if we must hate. Let's discriminate against discrimination if we have to discriminate. Let's show prejudice against prejudice if we are to be prejudiced. Let's direct our entire stereotype against stereotypes if we choose to typecast. Then, man could hate all he wants, discriminate as he likes, prejudice as he deems, and stereotype at his pleasure. How beautiful the world would be if whites could confront whites about prejudice and people of color challenge vindictive folks. Wouldn't the world be a wonderful place if real Christians halted the stereotypes among them and nonviolent Muslims had the courage to speak up against those who kill in the name of God? The world would lose its body, spirit, and soul to evil if fine men, women, and children stay silent when it mattered.

There have been three categories of men and women in the course of human history: those who were against evil and did something about it, those who were against evil but did nothing about it, and those who embraced evil and did everything to advance it. Where a man or a woman stands in the course of history determines the quality of memory that lives after him or her. Posterity would remember three grades of men and women: those who did something, those who did nothing, and those who cuddled evil. Where do you and I stand, KKK? The ultimate places for our memories depend on if we made the world a better or bitter place. I passionately pray that we should make the world a better place.

What happens to the children, who we so much loved, if we bequeath an intolerably hostile world to them? Where were the pious when the impious gave faith a bad name? When would man understand that violence breeds nothing except a vicious circle of violence? Why did tolerant people shut their mouths when bigots took over the world? How many ground zeroes should the world tolerate before tackling religious chauvinism?

I have a mission. KKK, you have a task. Both of us need to remake the world. Our offspring must not inherit a treacherous world when we are done and gone. Not only would hatred of the people by the people and for the people deny our children happiness, it would also zap their children's delight. The coming generations fall victim when all-conquering forces engage insurmountable forces in a war of attrition. Can't we all just get along when some could no longer force others to distant planets?

"We love our children to death," we insist.

But how much love do we really have for them when we care less about how many enemies we make for them in our lifetimes? Many are buying life insurance policies so their loved ones could live happily ever after. What good is this when we leave countless crevices uncovered along the beneficiaries' paths? Our children are ill-fated if they have to travel long hours and lengthy distances by road because the enemies we left for them are good at generating doomed airplanes. It is most unfair to our offspring if we limit their freedom and desire to explore because our actions created cultures and neighborhoods that they could not step. KKK, we cannot afford to neglect prejudice, discrimination, and stereotypes.

We may consider fortifying our children with all-conquering forces, so they could surmount their enemies, but the world is no longer as conventional as it used to be. Firepower is no longer an absolute deterrent against willpower. Guns are no longer good restraints against those who care less about living. We have everything to lose, but the enemy has little to lose. Those who have nothing to lose care less about offending those who set fires. Did we reflect on the contemporary, obstinate Lilliputians that our offspring would face? The diminutive creatures, like every living thing, have the will to survive and even become overwhelming. Imagine how overpowering a company of tiny ants is to a huge python that strays into their region. Life may not be fun for our children if they have to spend their lives contending with mighty forces confronting insurmountable, little forces.

It alarms me to think that our children might, once again, contend with the enemies that believe they have nothing to lose, that is, those who give their lives so others might die. KKK, now that we have the option, I passionately hope you and I would find a way to restructure the world.

Man sometimes embraces irrationality instead of rationality in his formative years. He listens to the voice of egotism instead of the voice of reason. He boasts and roasts his chance of demonstrating maturity. Now, we are old and ripe with responsibilities, KKK. We must do things differently. The elderly does not celebrate carelessly like the uninitiated. Grown people who fail to do things differently have not—and would never—grow up. Let elderly whites reach out to their youths and tell them that hatred is not a virtue. People of color must inform their young ones that hatred creates no prosperity. It is the responsibility of grown men everywhere to tell their sons that there is more to life than hating others. Full-fledged women in all cultures should encourage their daughters to care about fellow humans, regardless of their colors, faiths, or groups.

Nothing is wrong with Christians, Muslims, and Jews returning to their roots to learn about times past. The books indicate that Abraham, an ally of God, was the ancestor of the founders of the renowned three religions. It is the peak of intolerance if Abraham's children cannot stand one another. It is a huge insensitivity to Abraham's memory if the three brothers cannot get along. The one who cherishes love among Abraham's children should reach out to his brothers. For instance, consider how I'm reaching out to KKK. Someone should edify young Christians, Muslims, and Jews that they have the same grandfather. Buddhism, Hinduism, Kabbalah, Shintoism, Bahaism, Sikhism, Scientology, Zoroastrianism, and Unitarianism have love and compassion in their diverse lingoes. Why should the various faiths fail to extend love and compassion to all of mankind? Why can't men recognize all of the clear reasons why they should celebrate diversity?

It is puzzling when faithful adherents kill in the name of an affectionate, caring, and forgiving God. Surprisingly, those who do not forgive fellow humans' shortcomings constantly ask God to look the other way when they err. The brainteasers of our time misappropriate God's will by killing fellow men for their sins without granting them the opportunity to repent. It is reasonable to conclude that God would be pleased with the faithful who guide sinners to salvation instead of killing and denying them the chance to atone. Man plays the deity when there is no god but God. No human is God. All—black, white, male, female, young, old, rich, poor, upright, and perverted—are mere mortals.

It sounds logical to assume that man kills sinners when he becomes lazy and unable to win souls for his faith. But he wants the world to see him as an authentic believer. KKK, you are probably wondering why I made such sweeping assumptions. I'm convinced that God would appreciate the man who wins souls with prayer, kindness, forgiveness, meekness, generosity, patience, and love. Regrettably, it is easier for the indolent faithful, like those who hate nature, to uproot trees instead of trimming, grooming, and nurturing them until they become elegant woods. Who is man to determine sinners when no one is clean before God?

KKK, why does man find another man objectionable? Can you tell what man really wants? Why do we clash without ceasing? Why do we unite when it suits our purposes and split effortlessly like feeble boats at the mercy of a violent ocean? Why do we run into discord so easily, just like frail trees that bend and shatter in the presence of a rampaging hurricane? Can't we just stick together when malevolence stirs the fire of revulsion among us? Shouldn't we just quit acting like mature beings sometimes and behave like children at other times? Is it too much for all to respect, rediscover, and compliment one another? We have reasons to humble ourselves and learn from each other.

There are no winners when we fight for superiority. Not only is the truly superior great in knowledge, he also has consideration, humility, and reverence for others. Thoughtfulness is the furthermost attribute of a superior mind. A superior one acknowledges that he does not know it all, but he knows he has something to learn from others. Anyone who claims to be superior without meekness, respect, consideration, and regard for others' achievements, is an impostor and bully. The truly superior mind, therefore, does not brag. The world is a system where all work together like the diverse parts of an engine. No piece of an engine is superior because all work together in unison. All parts of the body work together. Every part becomes uncomfortable when a part of the body becomes uncomfortable. The diverse parts of the world play varied roles to make the whole work. The assorted cultures and endowments were to compliment each other. It is the varied parts of a system, not the individual components that make it superior.

More friends are better than more enemies. Simply, more of good things are better than more of bad things. Additional good friends mean additional goodwill, but extra enemies mean extra malice. More goodwill adds pleasure to life. More malice takes away contentment from life. We must choose the best for our children. Giving pride the leeway to prod us toward hatred will surely rob our offspring the goodwill they need. Pretending all is well in the face of an anxious world is not prudent. Hoping that our children would take care of the problems themselves is not discreet either. Rather than transferring abhorrence to our children, we must clean up after ourselves. KKK, you and I should embark on the mission of making tomorrow better.

We have our future in our hands. We have distinct choices before us. We have the option of fighting for superiority or fighting against inferiority. We could sustain the war of attrition started by those before us or liberate our minds from the shackles of intolerance. If we so desire, we could leave time bombs for those coming after us or make the world a free place for them. I have always thought that our children deserved true freedom. They merit the liberty to travel the world unrestrained instead of localizing themselves to some terrains they have seen repeatedly. There is true freedom on earth when your children have full access to my territory and my children are uninhibited in your district. This makes sense, and it appeals to me.

Let's reflect more altruistically, KKK. Where is man's supremacy when he does not understand unity in diversity? How superior is the mind that fails to comprehend that all is possible when people sum up their strengths and not their pettiness. What does it matter if a man sees a snake and a woman stops it from hurting people? Should man sulk over who stops the venomous serpent from hurting children? Who cares about which culture discovered what? Our collective goal should be the pursuit of happiness for all of mankind. Egg or chicken, it does not matter which came first. Man needs both for his pleasure. Cultural achievements are not limited to particular groups. The Nile Valley was the cradle of civilization, but mankind's progress did not end with the pyramids. It is too early in the history of mankind to tell which culture would discover what next.

Man is not superior or sophisticated enough if insensitivity toward others, ground zeroes, and carnage are what we get from the knowledge we acquired, the faiths we embraced, and the associations we keep. We cannot talk about superiority when we lack the capacity to solve man-made hatred with the knowledge that man possessed. Advanced minds are for solving problems, not inordinate boasting about the gifts of nature. Superiority becomes a synonym for inferiority when it becomes petty, egotistical, and odious. Any group of mankind cannot obtain superiority until people of color, white, agnostic, faithful, upright, and perverted people overcome the petty challenges of hatred and egoism. Until then, superiority belongs to a power beyond man's reach.

Sensible people everywhere are tired of racially motivated revulsion, faith-based hatred, and gang warfare. Racism is uncharitable. Religious hatred is an affront on divinity. Gang warfare is the only option left for a coward. The world does not need anymore mass graves. We cannot afford to breed additional orphans. Let's transform the killing fields to healing fields where no one dies. Instead, people heal and forgive one another. Let's turn ground zeroes to ground heroes, where men and women stand for what is right. There is a connection between heroes and the body, soul, and spirit of mankind. Heroes do not hate on behalf of their races. They do not kill for their religions. They do not share affiliation with mischievous gangs. They place others first. "People" is the name of their religion. Humanity is their gang's nomenclature. Heroes give themselves to the services of others, regardless of their skin colors, faiths, and associations.

Mother Teresa, Lady Diana, Rosa Parks, Mahatma Gandhi, Martin Luther King Jr., Anwar Sadat, and Pope John Paul II were heroines and heroes of their times. They stood for unity and respect for all of mankind. They were proud members of their races, but they were heroic enough to love the world. They were committed to their beliefs, but they were sincere enough to believe in mankind. They cherished the associations they belonged, but they gave their loyalties to humanity.

Nelson Mandela, Jimmy Carter, the Dalai Lama, Bill Gates, Gani Fawehinmi, Oprah Winfrey, Daw Aung San Suu Kyi, Bono, and Bob Geldof are some of the heroes and heroines of our time. They have races, beliefs, and associations, but they do not turn their backs on the world. They are the consciences of the world and the trustees of a better tomorrow.

KKK, you and I could become heroes and goodwill advocates of our time, too. We could turn bad to good if we so desire. The distance between bad and good is the "and" between them, just as the distance between black and white is the "and" that separates them. Whites, blacks, Hispanics, Native Americans, Asians, Alaskans, and Pacific Islanders would become one if they remove the commas that separate them. Then, we would have a true melting pot in this world. We could emulate past and present heroes and heroines by building bridges among peoples and cultures. We could turn hate parades to unity processions. It is okay for hoodlums to steal our racial hoods. We could make waves by telling the young ones complimentary stories about one another. We could even get together and introduce our children to each other as relatives because you and I are distant brothers.

CHAPTER 2

▼

FORGOTTEN LINEAGE

The universal brotherhood of man is our most precious possession.
—Mark Twain

KKK, we are not ordinary acquaintances as we thought. You'll be amazed to know that all humans are real brothers and sisters who share one destiny. Let us retrace our steps and orient ourselves about the forgotten lineage, that is, our common ancestry. We need to remember our past odyssey because our current heritage has held us hostage enough. How long will today prevent us from remembering our shared yesterday? Our lack of memory has dazzled us brothers and prevented us from seeing one another clearly. Now the time has come for man to meet himself. Read carefully now as I tell you the story of mankind's journey from Africa—the story that links you and I as brothers.

In the beginning, our ancestors were brothers. Researchers say they lived together in Africa thousands of years ago. We assume their skins were dark because they lived around the equator. Researchers theorized that the climate conditions of that age were intimidating. Thus, a group of the brothers migrated, leaving those of their brothers who decided to weather the storms in Africa. The migrants headed northeast through the present-day Middle East. They reportedly made themselves new homes around the Arabian isthmus until further circumstances made a portion of them migrate southeast toward modern-day India. Whatever circumstances originally motivated the people to start the big journey continued for many years after. A segment of the people continued the migration odyssey, possibly traveling on primitive rafts and canoes across the ocean to Southeast Asia and Australia, daring whales, sharks, and other feral creatures. As people migrated, some put down roots along the way, forming the beginnings of the populations of many regions of the world.

How did the brothers aboard those primordial ocean rafts feel as they struggled for their lives? They had no idea where they were heading, but they did not forget where they were from. They had nothing but each other. Fate joined them together as brothers. They needed one another to survive as they traveled at the mercy of a tempestuous ocean and monstrous water animals. They probably survived by sticking to one another throughout the arduous journeys.

Brother KKK, I wish you and I could imagine the support and love that these people shared. I desire that mankind could relive the sincerity and goodwill that those brothers shared. They must now be so disappointed that their descendants despise each other and wish one another death.

Brother KKK, I can tell that you are beginning to warm up to the story of how our ancestors were brothers and how you and I became brothers as well. Researchers explain further that some of the African peoples later migrated to Europe. The great journey continued because man's instinctive desire to evade hazardous weathers or seek after greener pastures probably did not allow many of them to tarry in a region forever. How did some of the migrants get to the new world? Researchers suggest they moved to North America possibly through Alaska. Perhaps they passed before the land passageways disappeared under the Arctic and Pacific Oceans. Maybe they moved across some gigantic, frozen ocean route. That must have been the chilliest and rockiest journey ever. In all probability, the ever-changing circumstances could have made some of the people migrate farther, to South America, the Caribbean, and the Pacific islands. Humans are migratory lots.

Researchers could not have made up the story, Brother KKK. You and I are brothers. The scientists have fine reasons to stand by their story. They have been to every region of the world, and they have retraced mankind's steps to Africa. Genetic material helped to prove that all of mankind came "out of Africa." Genetic science does not disagree about our lineage. I am convinced that we are brothers, notwithstanding the different skin pigmentations. Our skin colors may be different, but that is another story entirely. Remember, our ancestors who stayed behind in Africa kept their dark skins. Their brothers, that is, those who moved away, developed lighter shades of colors, depending on where they stopped. Thereafter, the diverse groups have been handing their genes to their offspring.

The voyage of our ancestors, the early brothers, around the world could not have been more inspiring. It was the most touching tale of survival, the utmost account of support from man to man, and the furthermost chronicle of love among brothers that had nothing but hope. Adults and children did not have anything except hope to survive. They were there for each other as long as they could go. These people were determined to float or sink together. They did not have any luxury of despising each other. They did not have any cause to wish death on one another. They simply needed each other. The unfriendly weather, hostile waters, and homicidal animals were enough to keep them busy. It is appalling that modern generations, who have good reasons to keep the ideals alive, find it difficult to get along.

It has been a while since our ancestors, the earliest brothers, departed from each other. But should we lose touch with our lineage? Should we stop caring about each other because we started living apart a while ago? Why do we detest each other on the basis of skin color? Why do we create chasms between us because of religion? Why do brothers alienate brothers because of gangs? Why do we allow class to classify us?

This is our moment of moral crisis, Brother KKK. Hatred is ripping through our world, like a warring tornado, wrenching brothers apart from brothers, and jerking sisters away from sisters. Violence of the people by the people and for the people is mustering strength to ruin our beautiful earth. Like a huge iron curtain, eloquence of prejudice is separating mankind from civility. Our children are listening to the disparaging stories we tell about each other, and we continue to dig gorges between our offspring.

Brother KKK, did you have the hunch, like I did, that we failed our departed brothers and sisters too soon after the 9/11 tragedy? No innocent and defenseless people should have to depart like they did ever again. They must be wiser for the cruel experience that fellow humans imposed on them. They would not want mankind to do another macabre dance on the edge of hatred. The departed must be asking you and me why we failed to sustain the tempo of the unity we found on 9/11. We need to talk, Brother KKK. And now is the time. Let's engage sound reasoning and see the abyss we are digging between ourselves. The time is right to remove the wool from our eyes and see the toll that conflicts are taking on our today and our children's tomorrow.

Let's end racial, faith, and gang-based hatred. Let tolerance ring. It is time to quit mimicking childish siblings who struggle over inconsequential issues when they should be watching each other's back. Our wounded today must not become our children's unhealed tomorrow. We could be Africans, Americans,

Arabs, Asians, Australians, Europeans, Jews, or Middle Easterners and remain humans. It is understandable to be Christians, Muslims, Jews, Buddhists, Hindus, agnostics, rich, or poor and respect one another. Brother KKK, we have the choice of acting like brave men or stark cowards. We are courageous when we begin to instruct our children that hatred is not a virtue, but we are cowardly when we insist there is virtue where there is none. I know that you and I are not cowards, Brother KKK. A coward is the bystander who watches quietly as wrong takes the place of right in the course of history. Even when those who support the wrong threaten to hurt us, we must stand by the right. Whoever avoids getting hurt by standing with the wrong would forever have his conscience mortally injured.

Our world owes it to posterity to take a break from decadence and stand by civility. Neutrality must take the place of bias. Responsibility must replace fanaticism. Subjectivity should wane. Objectivity must soar above the inequitable perception of one man by another. "Live and let live" should not become a cliché in a world with large skies. The world is big enough for diverse birds to fly freely without ruffling each other's wings. Our children should have an enhanced world, one that is devoid of the acts of intolerance that our generation and those before us fashioned. What purpose will it serve if we bequeath a precariously polarized world to our offspring, Brother KKK? Without uprooting the tree, let's harvest the leaves enough for our use so our children could have something to thrive on. Polarizing the world amounts to uprooting the tree of life.

Christianity, Islam, Hinduism, Buddhism, Judaism, Shintoism, Bahaism, Sikhism, Scientology, and Zoroastrianism are variants of worship by mankind. They recognize peace in their varied doctrines. Why does man use the religions that identify with compassion as launching pads for hatred? All seven continents are integral parts of our planet. Why should the people from these regions, who originated from one source, turn against each other, like lower animals in the jungle? Race, religion, class, and association are not the problems. It is the agents of polarization who use the groupings to pitch man against man.

Brother KKK, it is logical to suppose that nature created the different regions of the world with diverse people, landmarks, vegetations, and weathers to complement each other. The man from Liverpool does not appreciate Hawaiian waters because there are no such waters in Liverpool. He simply appreciates diversity, that is, the fact there are bodies of water elsewhere. The American woman who appreciates the Serengeti Plain does not do so because there are no wildlife sanctuaries in America. She prefers variety. People and groups must accept the common destiny of being parts of a diverse world. Diversity has been an important topic at different forums for a while. It is time to celebrate it.

Even though the quantities of melanin in our skins differ, we profess diverse faiths and belong to different rungs of the prosperity ladder. Mankind has more in common than all that separate us. We speak diverse words, but we belong to one world. There are different faiths in the world, but we share one fate. We are one people shackled together by fortune. We are a herd of bulls yoked together by providence. We are diverse groups of people without the luxury of diverse destinies. Our common survival is only possible when we work together. Going our different ways would wrench energies from us. Consequently, we may never reach our collective goals. We are members of one world with one destiny. We could save our children and ourselves only by learning how to survive together as brothers and sisters.

Who is a brother, Brother KKK? A brother watches the back of his brother. A brother does not turn his back because he could. A brother does not walk away when one has difficulties. Brothers are not arrogant because of the favors they do one another. They do not hate or stereotype one another. Brothers do not bring each other down. Brothers do not call each other names. Brothers do not tell their children disparaging stories about one another. Real brothers do not engage in violence to settle differences. Brothers who do so are evil. Evil is despicable. Whatever is evil is not virtuous. A good brother is everything, for example, an affectionate father, counselor, teacher, minister, confidant, and advocate. If you have a good brother, you have a loyal ally. I wish we could become good brothers and loyal allies, Brother KKK.

We have gone through hard-hitting challenges, but that should not stop us from being brothers. From my experience, I learned that only one thing in life is permanent, and that is change. I have seen worst enemies become best friends and best friends turn into worst enemies. With some tact, the archenemy today might become the closest ally tomorrow. Remember Germany, Italy, and Japan during World War II? They were America's archrivals. As providence would have it, they are now some of America's friends. Every wise man refrains from taking worldly issues personally. That's why I resolved to reach out to you, Brother KKK. My love for you remains. I hope to see all of mankind becoming close allies.

Our ancestors' voyage from Africa to the rest of the world was a piece of man's journey. Mankind's trip continues as long as nature tolerates or as long as we tolerate one another. Nature did not bear with our ancestors, but they supported each other. The unfriendly environments of that age did not tolerate them, but they tolerated one another by sticking together and arriving at new destinations. Our ancestors stood together against nature and survived.

Our survival depends on our ability to tolerate one another, like our original ancestors did. Mankind is now capable of influencing unfriendly environments, but we have unfriendly mentalities to tackle, including hatred, prejudice, and stereotypes. The unfriendly mind-sets of our time could stop us from reaching new heights. We must not allow unfriendly mentalities to terminate our existence when unfriendly environments could not stop us.

Brothers may not necessarily be equal. They may have diverse preferences and ideas. They may be poles apart on the prosperity ladder. They may even see the world through different prisms. Regardless, brothers are brothers because more things unite them than all that separate them. We may be different, like the diverse trees that make up the forest, but we share the same roots. There are woods and shrubs, tall and short plants, broad and diminutive foliages, as well as thick and moderate bushes with varied hues and textures. But all of them entangle to make the jungle. Tall trees are not necessarily more potent than short shrubs because all trees have their diverse uses and importance. Just like a shrub does not make a jungle, a tree does not make a forest. trees and undergrowth complement each other and make up the forests. We have a lesson to learn here, Brother KKK.

Just like whites do not account for all of mankind, people of color do not constitute the world. Like assorted trees and shrubs make up the forest, all colors, religions, classes, and genders make up the world. An abundance of diverse creatures is the most amazing thing about creation. Our planet would not be worth its existence without the skies, waters, mountains, valleys, plateaus, prairies, forests, deserts, and living things complementing each other. Boredom would asphyxiate the minds that exclude themselves from the rest of the world. By creating variety, diversity was nature's deliberate attempt to reduce boredom among mankind. Boredom has to do with seeing the same thing, doing the same thing, and having limited options over a period of time.

Bigots see adversity in diversity, but I see variety. Variety comes with options. Options provide freedom. A diverse world that guarantees worldwide brotherhood of mankind provides real freedom. I am talking about a world that assures the freedom of whites in people of color neighborhoods and assures the liberty of people of color in white quarters. I want a world where Muslims are not second-class citizens in Christian nations and Christians get respect in Islamic nations. I crave a world where "I disagree with you" should not become "I hate you." Freedom has no place in the lexicon of a people who watch their steps in their own countries and own world. Freedom means visiting wherever you choose and whenever you want without fear or hindrance. Racial, faith, and gang-motivated restrictions are some of the essential characteristics of captivity.

Placing men and women's minds in bondage, including racial and religious groups, puts man in the past. A people that shackle the minds of good men and women to ethnic, faith, and union poles cannot boast of being a part of a modern world. Retroactive attachment to goodness differs from obstinate attachment to backwardness. Only oppressive individuals, nations, and cultures tolerate those who draw racial and religious boundaries among the people. Any nation that allows a man's freedom to cause pain for another man remains ancient, no matter the level of advancement she professes.

How advanced is our world when individuals, groups, and cultures are yet to tolerate one another? It is pathetic that cultural boundaries are thicker than national boundaries in our cities. It is such a pretentious world when nationals disagree among each other than with the citizens of another country. It is appalling when people who ascribed to be parts of a nation discriminate against each other. How can people claim to dwell in an indivisible nation when the qualities of life depend on the sides of the economic divides they belong to? How united is a nation when adults bawl at youths for crossing cultural lines?

Brother KKK, I long to see my children inviting your children to my neighborhood. I would encourage my offspring to visit your children without apprehension. I hope to raise my children with enough room in their hearts to host mosaics of friends from the diverse cultures of the world. I would instruct my children to be proud of whom they are, but I want them to celebrate who their friends are. My offspring would be pleased with their nationality, but they would accept the whole world as their constituency. They would bear their faith with dignity, but they would profess people as their religion. I will teach them to be proud of the group they belong to, but they should claim their membership to the human race above all other associations. I pray you are on board with me in these regards, Brother KKK.

Let's suppose that the unexpected happens as we teach our children what we know about life, but they find out that we were wrong. What if my children accuse me of misleading them into disrespecting other cultures and your offspring accuse you of tricking them into hating innocent people? What if something deep inside keeps agitating them and we cannot convince the next generations that we did everything possible to teach them charity? You and I know very well that we need to edify them with goodwill. Are we prepared to look directly at our progeny and tell them that we misled them naïvely? If we really care, we have the chance to make things right now.

We could pretend that all is well if we divide the world, but you and I know that the truth remains constant. The certainty remains that hatred did not solve problems yesterday. It is not solving any problems today, and it would not resolve any problems tomorrow. He who hates does not hurt the hated person alone. He hurts himself as well. Haters poison their souls when their bodies release the toxin of hatred. They torture their spirits as well when they unknowingly unleash guilt on their essence. The painful part yet is that haters do not heave the burden of revulsion on themselves alone. They haul it on the innocent generations that accept the culture of hatred harmlessly. The transfer of hatred to innocent hearts is the worst injustice we could do to our progeny.

Brother KKK, giving and taking a little of love would make the world a better place. Giving and taking a little of the loathing would make the world a bitter place. What good is hatred today when it did not do any good yesterday? How would our children get along tomorrow if you and I do not get along today? What future waits for mutually opposing generations of people whose ancestors bequeath nothing but hatred? You and I know that an eye for an eye would make all of us blind in no time. What chance do our children have if our actions have been laying hostile mats of mutual destruction for them to sleep on? Maybe we have been leading our children along the immoral path innocently.

I hope we could banish hatred from our "what to do" list and say good riddance to the bad rubbish called discrimination. I wish the world were filled with brothers who are not necessarily siblings or members of the same race. I yearn to see all men, women, and children professing love as their religion, compassion and their song, and brotherhood as the essence of their catechism. I crave for a world where man's fate does not stop him from having faith in fellow men. I desire to see a free world devoid of prejudice, religious bigotry, and associations based on hatred. I envision a universal brotherhood of men, women, and children where race, color, and class do not determine memberships. I entreat mankind to get there soon.

Brother KKK, I wish for the brotherhood of all of mankind from all sovereignties and protectorates. I am asking for a united America where tolerance, trust, and respect are all-time tenets and adversity is not the uniting factor for the diverse peoples. I am asking for a peaceful Middle East where the nations sheath their swords and take their places among progressive nations. I am soliciting Africa, the ancestral home of mankind, to be a place where conflicts have no place in a person's glossary. I would like a cooperative Afghanistan, Pakistan, and

India. I would like for China, Taiwan, and Tibet to live in peace. I would insist on harmony among the Southeast Asian nations and forbid conflict between the two Koreas.

If magic were real, I would conjure a blissful world where camaraderie stretches throughout Australia, Brazil, Cambodia, Dominica, Egypt, and France. I would invoke understanding throughout Ghana, Haiti, Ireland, Japan, Kyrgyzstan, and Laos. I would juggle friendship through Mongolia, Nigeria, Oman, Portugal, Qatar, and Russia. People would care about people all over Seychelles, Turkey, Uruguay, Vanuatu, and Western Sahara. Xylophones of Yugoslavia and Zambia would sing of friendship forever. The Vatican and Mecca would exchange emissaries of goodwill. All faiths would be at peace with one another. Harmony, affection, and consideration for others would abound in every nation, kingdom, or monarchy.

Conflict incenses people and begets loss against the will of nature that gave so much to prosper man. The holy city of Jerusalem in the Middle East, for instance, was the cradle of some of the most remarkable heritages in the world. It was the root of Christianity, Islam, and Judaism and includes such sites like the Wailing Wall, the Church of the Holy Sepulcher, al-Aqsa Mosque, and the Dome of the Rock. The shrines of the dominant religions are short distances from each other. For the Jews, the Wailing Wall is their most revered place of worship. The Christians say that Jesus Christ was crucified and interred at the location of the Church of the Holy Sepulcher. The Muslims believe Prophet Mohammed ascended to heaven where al-Aqsa Mosque and the Dome of the Rock are. The Jews also believe God asked Abraham to sacrifice his son, Isaac, at the same site. The region should be taking advantage of the extraordinary heritages to make its fortune through tourism. Regrettably, the sacred city's challenges do not allow her to maximize her tourism potential because the people hardly get along. There is so much subjectivity. Each group wants the city instead of living and earning a fortune in brotherhood.

Close your eyes, Brother KKK. Picture how authentic nature really is. Envision the wide blue sky and the serenity it offers man. Visualize the azure ocean and the coolness it gives to the day. See the majesty of the hills by the sea and the splendor they grant the countryside. Think about the rolling evergreen pastures that cap the hills and carpet the prairies. Imagine the breathtaking waterfalls and free-flowing rivers that nature bequeaths to man. Perceive the abounding grandeur of nature in your mind's eye. The picturesque finery of the hills that pierce the velvety clouds and the blue skies are real. The vivid sight of the sea, hills, and horizon merging into picture-perfect exquisiteness cannot be more authentic.

The perfect-finishing nature that fashioned all of these wonders could not have created diversity by accident.

Nature leaves enough evidences wherever we look to show that nothing existed for which there was no purpose. But man has yet to discover the purpose. He who appreciates the day should compliment nature for the sun. Whoever loves the glow in the dark should not despise the moon. He who gazes into the night should commend nature for a million stars. Anyone in a state of boredom should praise nature for the choices that come with diversity. Mankind's assorted colors and diverse mores were deliberate acts of nature. I am of the same opinion as Mark Twain. Therefore, "The universal brotherhood of man is our most precious possession."

CHAPTER 3

▼

THE QUEST

Consider the following. We humans are social beings. We came into the world as the result of others' actions. We survive here in dependence on others. Whether we like it or not, there is hardly a moment of our lives when we do not benefit from others' activities. For this reason it is hardly surprising that most of our happiness arises in the context of our relationships with others.
—The Dalai Lama

Brother KKK, I reaffirm my quest for universal brotherhood of man. A few questions are begging for answers from you and me. We must not leave them for our children to tackle so they will not assume that we left the questions of intolerance, prejudice, and fanaticism for them to unknot because we were too indolent to unravel them. We classified those who lived before us as *Stone Age* because they were not sophisticated enough to craft aircraft. Centuries from now, how would it sound if our successors labeled us as *Smart but Silly*? I bet they would be astounded that we were clever enough to fabricate aircraft and even visit the moon, but we were not smart enough to get along. Our generation would have failed dismally if our wounded today becomes our children's unhealed tomorrow.

This is the time for heart-to-heart talk, Brother KKK. It is a point in time to take a stand for benevolence or malevolence. We may throw hard questions at each other, but we should not lose sleep over them. Our words could be compassionately muddy, but we should forgive one another if smeared. It is better to throw reasonable words at each other now than for our offspring to throw rocks at each other or for their children to throw missiles at one another. Engaging rational words for reaching each other's heart is not a bad idea. We could even exploit equitable parables when words are not enough. Parables are words' horses. People ride parables to search for words when the latter are missing. Brother KKK, I love and respect you. Now, let's get to work and ask some down-to-earth questions and provide heartfelt answers. This is all for our children's sake.

Who among us determined his skin color? What was our contribution to deciding our races? When are we going to comprehend that religions should not become instruments of hate? Why do we despise other groups because they are different? Why do we mischievously place colors and associations above our common ancestry? Why does man create gangs and allow his creations to rule his emotions?

Brother KKK, we did not commit anything into determining our skin color and contribute anything to becoming members of our races. Man did not profess any religions in the womb and claim any gangs inside his mother. The cultures he met in the world influenced his choices. Faith is the beautiful instrument of exaltation that agents of polarization exploit to promote personal agenda. A gang is the creation of disruptive losers who seek attention at all cost.

We found ourselves where we found ourselves! In truth, we could have been Africans, Americans, Arabs, Asians, Europeans, Hispanics, Indians, Jews, or Persians. We could have embraced Buddhism, Christianity, Hinduism, Judaism, Islam, or Shintoism! Circumstances could have bestowed other faiths on us. Nature could have created us as parts of the groups that we despised. Nature created man deliberately, but man did not choose his race.

If man's race is a game of chance, why do we hate? Why do we hurt each other over skin color? Why should we despise the men who could have been our brothers? Why should we scorn the women who could have been our sisters? Can't we just be a part of the solution, not a part of the dilemma that hunts mankind? How do we influence human causes in our times? Why should tragedy, not brotherhood, determine our unity? Isn't it better to make more friends than more enemies? It is time to reclaim our common ancestry. It is noble to restore trust and brotherhood among all of mankind.

Brother KKK, hatred does not have any race and does not belong to any particular religion. No culture owns a cartel of evil. No group has a monopoly of charity either. Haters propagate their odious agenda behind what man values, that is, race, religion, class, and ways of life. Each group has its own share of those who set brothers against brothers, children against parents, wives against husbands, and cultures against cultures. The agents of polarization are mere pretenders who veil their caustic scheme with racial, religious, and gang curtains. Their agenda is limited to converting the gorgeous world to a vicious planet where invincible forces remain in constant struggle against immovable forces. Our planet is in a steady state of conflict.

Terror is not limited to foreign cultures. Timothy McVeigh, the Oklahoma City bomber, killed fellow Americans because terrorists were not always foreigners. Eric Rudolph, the Olympic Park Bomber, engineered homegrown terror against his homeland. Ted Kaczynski, the Unabomber; Terry Nichols, another man associated with the Oklahoma City bombing; and José Padilla, an American who was convicted of lending support to al Qaeda, rebelled against their nation because terrorists don't care about their own homeland.

When it comes to senseless killings, Osama bin Laden and Ayman al-Zawahiri do not draw any line between fellow Muslims and infidels. They bump off everyone along their path because hatred does not respect any religion. Abu Mussab al-Zarqawi murdered innocent Muslims in Iraq because he had a personal agenda apart from religion. Japanese Chizuo Matsumoto, founder of the notorious cult Aum Shinrikyo (Aleph), did not flinch before releasing sarin gas inside a Tokyo subway. He was not a citizen of any of the countries associated with terrorism after all.

Whenever I look through the prism of reality, I see objectivity instead of subjectivity. I understand clearly that bigots see the world through the prisms of subjectivity rather than the prisms of objectivity. Man presumes to see well through the prism of subjectivity, but, regrettably, his own imperfection obstructs him. Hating another man for embracing a different religion is not objective. The latter's choice of faith may not even be his own making. Man's choice of religion sometimes goes beyond his choice. Family, nationality, personal conviction, persuasion, and circumstances influence people's choices of religions and groups. The Pope's brother is inclined to be a Catholic. The son of Mecca's Grand Imam is likely to be a Muslim.

Brother KKK, I have a riddle. Who has it all, yet must earn it all? The answer is man. He has all things before him when he is alive, but he leaves everything behind in death. He only takes the virtue he earned in his lifetime. It makes sense for man to fight only for what he can take with him. It is futile to fight over what we did not create and would not take with us to the great beyond. No man would take religion with him, but what he did with religion would speak for him. No one would take a piece of land with him either. I cannot think of anyone who would keep his skin color forever. The man who looks at religion through the prism of subjectivity is as shortsighted as the man who looks at land through the prism of subjectivity. Both suffer from objectivity degeneration.

There are no clear winners when man creates ground zeroes because of land. The longest-living humans own land only for a few scores of years before land owns them at the end of their journeys. Every landowner in history ended up inside land. It is most ironic when man fights over what owns him in the end. Maybe people fight over land to bequeath pieces of it to their children. Regrettably, no offspring enjoys the land on which his ancestors left many enemies.

What use is the land if younger generations spend the rest of their lives brawling over it? How contented are the beneficiaries of terrains bestowed by ancestors who earned packs of enemies in their lifetimes?

Brother KKK, I hope we are not making the earth a bed of jagged pebbles for our children as we bicker over nothing. Don't we care that the world would become a prickling carpet of thistles if we continue to sow thorny seeds everywhere? An impassioned and edgy world has nothing good in stock for our children. We must not pass on the man-made aggressions of our time to the coming generations. Remaining obstinate with ego pumping could relegate our children to the league of endangered species. Our failure to back out from this game of chicken is most ill advised. We can continue with this to the peril of the coming generations.

Let's confront the truth once, Brother KKK. Let's be sincere for a moment and allow subjectivity to wane for an instant. Let's tackle frankness right now and give objectivity a chance. We must agree that it takes the real man to bow for goodness and the dim-witted man to hang on to depravity. Let's stoop for the truth and agree we did not create the racial glory that we are taking. You and I came into the world through the works of others. We cultivate and exploit the free-given soils that we did not generate. We drain the free-flowing waters that we did not engender. We hunt the nature-given animals that we did not originate.

I seek not to brandish faith in this stance. Instead, I want to draw lines between objectivities and subjectivities. Can man be certain that he represents the Divine when he kills infidels in the name of a God that detests killing? How dare man slay fellow men on behalf of the most affectionate and all-forgiving God? Who has seen the mind of God and could definitely say how he plans to judge the earth? Who is man to define the guilty with all certainty when every flesh is presumed imperfect before the Almighty? What if the Divine is not pleased with those who deny sinners the chance to atone for their shortcomings before terminating their lives? Consider the self-appointed faithful who take fellow humans' lives on behalf of God and against his command that man should not kill. It is fair, therefore, to suppose that these men are murderers.

How ill-advised and depraved are those who hate over the skin color they did not invent? It is immoral when man becomes a bigot over race. By no means should we ever be proud of intolerance of the people, by the people, and for the people. We cannot boast of a meaningful civilization when intolerance is taking the place of civility. Real civilization only comes when man uses other people's dispositions, not the hues of their skins, as the yardsticks for measuring them. Man can speak of genuine progress only when the faithful introduce their faiths to others with tenderness instead of intimidation. Cultural advancement is attainable only when cultures understand and respect cultures.

Violence would wane if all cultures appreciated the value of human life. Mankind would live in peace if societies discouraged agents of destabilization. Countries would exchange camaraderie if stronger nations became impartial judges and shelved double standards. Understanding would thrive in the world if nations did not gang up, to the exclusion of others, for selfish reasons. Mankind would be free from the menace of annihilation when man would harness knowledge for problem-solving endeavors only. Proliferation of weapons of mass destruction betrays man as a compulsive pretender that speaks from both sides of his mouth. He speaks of peace with one side of his mouth and transacts arms deal with the other. This is unquestionably reckless!

Mankind would live in harmony everywhere if we would renounce hatred and shun violence. The heavens would be delighted if we would not litter the space with armaments. Women and children would be saved on the hillsides when man would stop burying explosives in them. Lands would be relieved if man would stop soaking them with fellow man's blood. The pastures would have fewer pollutants if we would stop contaminating them with unstable elements. Waters would be purer when the radioactivity of our weapons would no longer slip into the channels. Above all, our children would be healthier and safer. Maybe man would learn how to solve problems creatively if all resources would go into peaceful use.

We can do the math, Brother KKK. Imagine the time, energy, materials, money, and lives that man commits into hostile endeavors. The time wasted is usually in multiples of the time we need to stop the conflicts. The exhausted energy exceeds what we need to soothe hurting nerves prior to fighting. Man could solve much of the problems that plague mankind if he would set aside the materials squandered on hostility for that purpose. The citizens of countries that go into war could use funds positively instead of committing them into senseless wars. Many families would not grieve if man would not go into wars against fellow men. It is so hopeless when man invests so much in killing fellow man. The vicious circle of suspicion and hatred that follow wars would not befall man if we would exercise restraints in the face of irritation.

I seek not to be politically correct. Instead, I would like to be conscientiously right. I am inclined to say that man's mind-set of "dog eats dog" will only lead him to the dog pound. Our flawed choice of "rat race" in place of "human race" is a bad omen. We are on our way to becoming illogical adults if we hope that our aggravation would reposition our children in the future. Mankind's fascination by pride is immature. Our obsession with ego is rash. Our infatuation with dominance will only aggravate rather than alleviate the coming generations. Let our generation take responsibility for our destabilizing actions so our children can make their own choices in liberty and take responsibility for their actions, too. It is fair for the coming generations to take responsibility for their actions only, not ours.

It is cruel, selfish, and dim-witted if we make enemies at our pleasure today that would make life miserable for our children tomorrow. It will be unkind, unjust, and unwarranted for our actions to place our children in harm's way. The acceptable option is to come to an agreement with the coming generations, giving them the honor of becoming the hope of tomorrow and trustees of a peaceful future. You and I cannot look at our children directly and say we passed hatred to them, but we knew it did not have any virtue. It takes someone with a huge heart to retract the thoughts of hatred to his children. Only a person with conscience takes back the prejudice he passed on to his offspring. Let's take back the intolerance we fed our children and pull out the derogatory stories we told them.

I will impart the philosophy to my children that it is all right to be an African and have white friends. They will learn that it is fun to have American, Arab, Asian, Australian, European, Jewish, and Persian friends. I will instruct them not to mistrust everyone who fails to make eye contact with them because not every culture values eye contact. My young ones will be skilled at accepting others because life is not about us against them. They will stand out because they will resolve issues peacefully. I will teach my children about integration and make them understand the dangers of disintegration. I will encourage them not to dwell on what they dislike about others. I will tell them to look for what is good about them. I implore you to do the same, Brother KKK.

My children will embrace their faith, but they should respect other faiths. I will teach them that it is okay to be Christian and have Jewish and Muslim friends. They will understand that Christianity, Islam, and Judaism have Abraham as their common ancestor. I will assure my children that people will appreciate their faith when they see them loving, caring, and forgiving others. My little ones will learn that kindness, humility, forgiveness, and entreaty persuade sinners, but threatening and intimidating others drive wedges between people and faith. I will even tell my little ones that Christianity, Judaism, Islam, Hinduism, Buddhism, Shintoism, Bahaism, Sikhism, Scientology, Zoroastrianism, and Unitarianism did not matter in the wake of the American tragedy. The diverse peoples, faiths, and groups embraced and supported one another on 9/11. Above all, I will tell my children that it is not all about religion. Instead, it is what one makes out of religion that endears him to the Divine.

I am on a mission to become a valuable teacher, counselor, and role model to my children. They will not share affiliations with unproductive gangs. Instead, they will partake in responsible associations. I will discourage my children from joining groups that hate, but they will enjoy my support when they join benevolent organizations. My offspring will not have any business with groups that operate in the dark of the night. They will work with charitable unions that have nothing to hide. Any groups that operate in the dark and have things to hide are creepy. My children will learn how to respect other cultures, beliefs, ideas, and ways of life. They will understand that "I do not share your belief" is different from "I hate you."

Brother KKK, please teach your children all of the above so they would stand accountable for their actions and your conscience will not go on trial for their demeanors. We may not agree on issues, but it is not prudent for our children to disagree when we wanted them to, not because they intended to. Setting our offspring against each other is nothing short of setting them up for failure. Everyone loses when a resolute force engages in a war of attrition with a tenacious force. This is a reality of our time, and we must learn how to live with it. We cannot pretend that all is well when we create so many enemies for those we will leave behind. It is understandable when brothers engage in sibling squabbles, but it is incomprehensible when they transfer their grievances to their offspring.

How do we teach our children the truth when we do not comprehend the unsurpassed truth they need to know about? Diversity is a reality; reality is the truth. Without lying, our generation cannot tell the coming generations that we did everything humanly possible to tackle the attacks on diversity. We cannot assert that we gave all to place prejudice and fanaticism where they belonged. Posterity would assume that we gave up on extremism and intolerance because they were too difficult for us to tame.

How mischievous is the generation that gave free reign to fanaticism and prejudice to please egoism? We cannot force fanaticism to take the place of tolerance and egotism to swap place with altruism.

Some of the finest men and women who lived or continue to live on this planet invested so much in mankind because they thought it was a good idea. I guarantee they were not stupid. Mother Teresa would not have lived and died among the poor in Calcutta instead of wining and dining with kings and queens elsewhere. Lady Diana, the Princess of Wales, christened the Princess of Hearts by a multitude of admirers, would not have touched bedridden AIDS patients around the world. If diversity were not real, Martin Luther King Jr. would not have died so the women and children repressed by man could live in liberty. Pope John Paul II was Catholic, but he shook hands with the Grand Imams of Islam. The soldier of faith fought to the very end so there would be understanding among religions, cultures, and groups.

President John F. Kennedy said, "The wave of the future is not the conquest of the world by a single dogmatic creed but the liberation of the diverse energies of free nations and free men."

He simply articulated what he had to say at the expense of losing ground to his political foes.

Rosa Louise Parks, the mother of the modern-day civil rights movement, saw beyond the momentary persecution that her refusal to give up her seat cost her. She held onto her seat, but she lost her liberty so man would not prevent the coming generations from simply sitting.

Albert Einstein once insisted, "The world is a dangerous place, not because of those who do evil, but because of those who look on and do nothing."

Those who hate others in the guise of fighting for their people neither love nor fight for their people. They are simply hiding behind their people's interest and pursuing their own agenda. Those who understand love share it across the board. They do not limit love to a few. He who loves his people does not make enemies for his people.

Eric Hoffer warned mankind about this type of people: "We hate others when we hate ourselves. We are tolerant toward others when we tolerate ourselves. We forgive others when we forgive ourselves. We are prone to sacrifice others when we are ready to sacrifice ourselves."

Can we take anything away from the sages? They made themselves allies of reality and saw beyond their noses.

It is not in the character of a patriot who truly loves his people to allow his actions to earn resentment for his people. He who loves his people is a good ambassador of his people, and he wins goodwill for his people in any permissible way he can.

St. Basil said, "He who sows courtesy reaps friendship, and he who plants kindness gathers love."

Anyone who thinks this is further from the truth should sow cassava and see if he could reap plantain. It is not right for those who love their people to use them as an excuse for pursuing endeavors that lack virtue. It is not true that those who hate others love their own people either.

"If it is not right do not do it; if it is not true do not say it," warned Marcus Aurelius, the second-century Roman emperor and philosopher. Let's make the world a better place.

Listen to the ramblings of sages. Pay little attention to the eloquence of politicians. Think about what wise men and shrewd women say. Do not take to heart what those who earn a living through making big talks and sipping expensive champagne utter. Concentrate on the substance, not the trivial. We should think about all that unite us, not all that divide us, so the coming generations would not find this generation unbelievable.

Franklin Thomas cautioned, "One day our descendants will think it incredible that we paid so much attention to things like the amount of melanin in our skin or the shape of our eyes or our gender instead of the unique identities of each of us as complex human beings."

He that detests diversity cannot invalidate Aristotle's philosophy, which counseled mankind that "nature does nothing useless."

This is where you and I come in, Brother KKK. We are responsible for speaking, counseling, and warning our children about the dangers of fanaticism, intolerance, and rash associations. We owe the young ones the duty of grooming, guiding, and guarding. Else, they would talk to the wrong crowds, take counsel from immoral groups, and fail to heed the sages' warnings. Every group is liable for what their children become.

Dietrich Bonhoeffer said, "The test of the morality of a society is what it does with its children."

What favor is more than bringing our children in contact with the truth? Truthfully, man cannot fault nature. Diversity is a wonder of nature.

Without any reasonable doubt, nature created mankind in diverse groups to harmonize each other as the physical features that make up man's environment complement one another. Just as the physical environment would be plain and uninspiring in the absence of contrast, a world without colors would be bland and uninteresting. There are no islands among men. We are all here to impact each other's life. Man defends woman; woman comforts man. Adults shelter minors; minors give joy to adults. Humans look after the domestic animals; animals give companionship to humans. Imagine what the world would look like with one race of mankind and one species of animal inhabiting the bare and uneventful plains of the South Pole.

The different parts of the world provide diverse views of the earth for man's delight. Our world comprises of contrasting beauties. Without which, man would question why he is here. The moon and stars even appreciate darkness because they would remain lackluster heavenly bodies without the night. The magnificence of flora would be lost without spring. The bravura of waterfalls would not exist without the heights. Rivers would not flow without the slopes. Rainbows would not color the horizons without the synchronized actions of the sun and water droplets. The deeps would be devoid of teeming marine life without water. Man would not inhabit land if the sun, air, and water were not here. Man would be completely bored in the absence of diversity.

The sages have spoken. The wise have counseled. The shrewd have warned. The masqueraders have danced. Let's pray that their sons would dance like them. Fireflies have brought their babies into the world. Let's hope that they would glow in the night. Praying mantises now have their babies. The little ones must learn how to pray. The wise among mankind have bared their minds to save man from himself.

Let those that have ears hear. Let those who hear comprehend. Let those who comprehend act. If we change the prejudice paradigm to a tolerance model, we have nothing to lose, but everything to gain. The man who teaches his son to hate has not listened. The woman who teaches her daughter to despise has not acted on the sages' warnings. Prejudice must wither.

CHAPTER 4

▼

WITHER PREJUDICE

Everything that irritates us about others can lead us to an understanding of ourselves.
—Carl Jung

Brother KKK, there comes a time when a man's mind matures and desires some truth. Then realism struggles to take the place of idealism. There comes an instance in the life of a woman when her heart longs for a voyage, taking her away from all of the vanities she knew. My mind desires some truth. My heart wants to break away from inordinate pride. The time is right for us to talk about altruism. Someone may deceive others and get away, but no one deceives himself and gets away from himself. I will not deceive you, Brother KKK, because you are a part of me and I am a part of you. It is true that we have dwelled in self-deceit for so long and have opted for fantasy in place of reality. Now that we are aged and the world is asking for accountability from us, I think it is time to embrace pragmatism in place of radicalism.

Radicalism makes man stick to what lacks merit. But pragmatism allows man to stand by what is right, even in the face of adversity. Radicalism makes an adult act like a child at the marketplace. But pragmatism brings out the maturity in a man. Radicalism encourages one to defend what lacks merit, and it makes intolerance look sensible. Pragmatism brings out the ripeness and reasoning in man. You know that hatred, prejudice, and stereotypes have malevolence in common, but love, tolerance, and broad-mindedness have benevolence. A detrimentally radical mind stands by what he thoughtlessly holds to be the truth. The pragmatic mind stands by what he thoughtfully holds as the truth.

Brother KKK, I once again offer you my love as I proceed with what I self-lessly hold as the truth. When drawn from the sheath carelessly, the sword cuts and destroys its own house gradually, but it assumes it is destroying the casing that belongs to its owner. Mankind destroys himself haphazardly when he is drawn into wars of attrition, but he claims he is destroying his enemies from other races, religions, and gangs. How can fellow humans be enemies when we should be watching each other's back? Brothers are eliminating brothers over nothing except intolerance, vanity, and greed. We decimate one another over ethnicity, religions, and gangs. We forget that humans inhabit the same world and share the same fate and destiny. Man has yet to understand that the evil that one man throws to another man will return to the thrower some day. This will happen as long as the earth rotates and winds blow. Whatever one dumps at sea somewhere would return home someday, as long as oceans generate waves. What happens to "what goes around comes around"?

Brother KKK, why do we wrestle over race, skin color, faith, and gangs? Should a deity remind us that we brought nothing to the world and will leave with nothing? It is vanity when we entomb the man who lacked virtue in a gold casket at the end of his journey. The worms that eat man do not accept golden bribes. Somehow, the virtue and honor we leave behind are the only things we own in the grave.

Where is the virtue in fighting over race when we did not select our races? Is there honor in brawling over skin colors when the skin would become food for worms and plants at the end of our journey? How witty is it to clash over land when land owns us in the end? This is why the wise among us bequeath virtue and true honor to the world so people can remember them.

There is no honor in killing in the name of God. Detesting others in the name of race lacks good judgment. Hating others because of gangs is not shrewd. What if God is neither black nor white? Neither brown nor red? Neither *Blood* nor *Crip*? What if he pays attention to the tenderness of a man's heart, not how religious he is? What if God is interested in the contents of a man's character, not the color of his skin? What if he has no business with gangs and despises those who hurt in the name of association?

Those who seek vengeance on behalf of the Divine may not be doing God a favor after all. Those who presume they fully understand his ways may discover that his philosophy is different from man's agenda. Man equates human reasoning and interpretations to God's. He classifies his own judgments as those of the revered one.

Haters are the vulnerable members of their groups. They are the weakest links that want to feel better somehow. They feel good about themselves with the synthetic feeling that they are better than some people after all. Haters nurse egoism in the part of their brains where sound reasoning should be residing. Brother KKK, you and I have no reason to fit anywhere in the classification of haters. The hater's ego assures him that he knows more than he truly knows. His sense of self assures him how clever he is to the exclusion of others. But the truly clever man is the unassuming human being who understands how little he knows in the limitless space of universe and time. Acknowledgment of one's limitations and a deep sense of appreciation for the wonderful works of nature are essential parts of knowledge, which only the truly clever man possesses.

Something deep inside keeps reminding me that winners do not hate. Losers detest others on the basis of race, religion, and gang affiliations. Winners are too thoughtful to hate and too eventful to hurt. Consider victors like Mahatma Gandhi, Kwame Nkrumah, Martin Luther King Jr., Anwar Sadat, Cesar Chavez, Mother Teresa, Princess Diana of Wales, Pope John Paul II, and Rosa Parks. They belonged to a class of their own, as opposed to Adolf Hitler of the old Germany, Benito Mussolini of Italy, Nicolae Ceausescu of Romania, Idi Amin Dada of Uganda, Saddam Hussein of Iraq, and Samuel Doe of Liberia. Every man writes his own epigraph in his lifetime. Some carve venerable ones for themselves; others engrave discreditable ones for themselves. We have the liberty to inscribe memorable epitaphs for ourselves while we are still here, Brother KKK.

Champions like Nelson Mandela, Jimmy Carter, Desmond Tutu, Bill Clinton, Bill Moyer, Bill Gates, Oprah Winfrey, Gani Fawehinmi, Bono, and Bob Geldof support their races, beliefs, and "gangs," but a lot of their actions benefit humanity. They are the first among equals that promote mankind with their personal talents, resources, and energies. They are the givers without borders. These winners have little in common with Slobodan Milosevic of Yugoslavia, Charles Taylor of Liberia, Collor de Mello of Brazil, Sani Abacha of Nigeria, Alfredo Stroessner of Paraguay, and Baby Doc Duvalier of Haiti. Anyone who has the opportunity to influence his destiny but botches it is destined to ruin the opportunities before him.

Winners do not limit their horizons by confining themselves to minuscule comfort zones. The Wright Brothers could have manufactured bicycles so they could ride to nearby towns only. But the winners in them created airplanes so they could fly across oceans, deserts, and icy lands. They did not limit charity to miniature empires. They made the world their constituency. Winners think outside boxes and find allies beyond their races, religions, classes, and gangs. They are proud of their races and who they are, but they fight for the whole of mankind. Winners have virtue and honor. Charity remains their watchword. Care is their slogan. They do not invest in the petty and mischievous efforts called "divide and rule." Winners have large hearts. They are not afraid to cross borders.

On the other hand, losers have little hearts and carefully hold onto the little they have. They do not venture far from their own, and they fear roaming an open world.

Let's discard hatred, Brother KKK. We must not pay the debts associated with hatred. Haters are petty-minded everywhere. They lack the wits for reflecting on issues creatively, no matter the level of their knowledge. It takes the deep to unlock the central questions behind human existence. Small-minded thinkers may not unlock them. Petty minds would never figure them out. You and I could crack the code for getting along if we give one another the chance. He who must solve the puzzles that haunt humans must start by accepting that everything about intolerance stinks. Diversity was a deliberate act of nature for the benefit of mankind. Respect for one another is the way forward. "Live and let live" is the code for human's continued existence.

Those who love others are famous twice, but haters live miserably twice. The former live gloriously in their lifetimes, and people celebrate them in death. Their names live famously after them. Many of them are even larger in death than in life. Their nomenclatures breathe memorably after they are gone. Who then chooses to hate except he who knows little about the dishonor that trails hatred?

You and I should not be like them, Brother KKK. Haters cannot grip anything as large as the world because their sense of appreciation does not go beyond their compact groups. Those who love do not fear the challenges that the larger world poses. But haters seek the easiest ways out by crawling into their comfort zones, excluding the larger world. Lovers open up the world for the benefit of all, but haters break it into pieces to avoid the challenges associated with the wide world.

Compassionate people with goodwill for all are winners as well as truly knowledgeable people. Can we describe petty, narrow-minded, ignorant, and selfish bigots who do not value others as strictly knowledgeable people because they went to college? It is not prudent either to classify open-minded, compassionate, judicious, and selfless people who value others and know how to get along as illiterates because they did not pass through college? Reading, writing, and knowledge acquisitions are the underlining elements of education, but the truly knowledgeable and liberated man is the one who adapts the instructions he acquired into making the world a better place. Haters are the ill-fated, modern-day illiterates.

Brother KKK, I definitely know that prejudice leads to intolerance. Stereotypes breed nothing except hatred. Hatred, in turn, yields nothing except separation, suffering, and sorrow. Our children have nothing to benefit from hatred. Consequently, it is time for prejudice, stereotypes, bigotry, discrimination, injustice, intolerance, unfairness, and chauvinism to wither. It is time for tolerance to rule supreme. It is time for you and me to start telling our children the story of tolerance, not prejudicial tales. It is time for acceptance to take the place of abhorrence and charity to take the place of chauvinism. The time is right for us to start ripping down walls and begin building bridges between fractured constituencies.

The world would be so pleasant and cheery if man held unity parades in our cities instead of hateful processions. Imagine the difference it would make if we would love and care about one another. Visualize how stunning and serene the world would be if groups would appreciate and compliment each other instead of detesting and pulling one another down. Picture how pleasing the world would be if groups would value and respect each other instead of excluding and prejudging one another. Envisage how harmonious and pleasurable the world would be if compassion would take the place of viciousness. Above all, Brother KKK, envision how free and liberated our children's minds would be if stories of abhorrence would not pollute them.

Should we engage logic for a moment, Brother KKK? I would say no if you would ask if every member of your race was bad. I guess you would probably say no if I would ask you the same question. In the same manner, you and I would say no if someone would ask if all the members of your race or mine were good. Now we have something in common. All the members of your group are not bad. All the members of mine are not awful either. Conclusively, there are good and bad people in all groups. Consequently, I will not, in all sincerity, dismiss all the members of your group because a few of them offended me. I expect you to reason the same way if some of my folks offended you. Remember we remain brothers, despite what we believe. We could come to a logical conclusion that treating people as individuals is more sagacious than lumping them together in judgment. Adjudicating people on the basis of races, faiths, or groups would only make us mistreat the majority of good people in every group.

I have been there, Brother KKK. I understand it takes people with a tainted sense of judgment to arbitrate a group based on the actions of a few. You would understand where I am coming from when you read about my early days in

America. Suppose I start with the day everything went wrong. I took double whamming from the intolerance of man against man. A friend offered me a ride to where I could take a bus to an important appointment. My friend was hurrying so much that I had little or no chance to do anything when she arrived at my place. After she dropped me off, I realized I had forgotten my wallet at home. It was important for me to keep the appointment, but I did not have any money to ride the bus. Home was a long distance for me to trek. I would have been too late for the appointment if I had returned to fetch my wallet anyway. I thought I should board the bus and explain my predicament to the driver, promising to return to the bus stop later and give him the money.

Dressed very professionally, I was wrong to assume that the driver would see me as a responsible person who truly forgot his wallet at home. The white driver looked at me contemptuously as I explained the circumstance that left me stranded.

"Please, step off the bus or I'll call the cops," he said, turning his face away from my direction.

The driver's harsh retort appalled another black passenger, and he pleaded, "Look at this gentleman. He doesn't look like someone who would lie because of a few cents. I knew when you allowed a white, homeless man to board the bus without paying."

The driver justified his action quickly, "The white guy was homeless. This guy doesn't look like one."

The black man appeared too angry to continue with the argument. He brought out his wallet and paid my fare.

I assumed the bus driver was absolutely right about the fact that people should pay when boarding the bus. But was his judgment right after offering a free ride to someone like him? He had the authority to ask me to get off the bus, but I expected him to be professional, considering my story and conduct. If someone thought the bus driver was biased, my journey back home appeared more torturous. I borrowed some money from someone I met at the appointment. I was waiting for a bus at the bus stop when the unexpected happened.

Two white teenagers drove by. One stuck his middle finger out of the car window and yelled, "N——Go home!"

I felt so appalled because I did not know the teenagers and I did not offend them.

Moments after the initial shock, I asked myself, "Should the actions of a few whites make me judge the whole race as mean people?"

I knew it was wrong to assume a whole race was bad because a few of them offended me.

My story has not ended, Brother KKK. I soon had the opportunity to confirm that mean people were not limited to a group and every member of my race was not outstanding either. Soon after, I traveled to another city and witnessed a different form of human reaction. The long journey had completely worn me out, and I could not move my heavy luggage alone. I needed someone to help me as I struggled to move it to a nearby bus stop. Two potential helpers were in proximity, a black man and a white man. I approached the black man and asked for help. I assumed he was more likely to lend a hand, but I was wrong. He looked at me as if I were crazy and walked away without saying a word. Surprisingly, the white man offered to lend a hand, and I did not have to ask for his help.

I have also seen the ugly head of prejudice and the beauty of fairness at the workplace. I witnessed colleagues with the same amount of tenure as me receiving raises without hassles, but I fought before I got mine, even though I had performed better than many of my colleagues. I did not assume that all the members of the race of the man who failed to pay me were bad. Some of them actually fought on my behalf before I received my rights.

In another incident, I saw the negative appraisal that a supervisor made about me for the first time while I was reading my annual assessment. The boss detailed a downbeat story that a member of her race told about me. But she had not bothered to ask for my side of the story. To date, the female supervisor remains the only boss who wrote something negative about me. However, I prevailed. Some members of her race were among those who stood up and attested to my outstanding work habits. Whoever says that every member of a race is bad is completely wrong.

Brother KKK, do I need more stories to validate my belief that it is better to judge people as individuals, not groups? Based on experience, I have learned to judge people on the basis of their characters, not their skin colors. A river of prejudice flowed past me before, but I struggled to observe, think, and make my own judgments without submerging in the obnoxious stream of hatred. Stereotypes tried to knock me to the ground with fairy tales of prejudice against others, but I was conscious of the fact that they were wrong. I knew that all whites were not racists and all blacks were not criminals. I recognized that all Hispanics were not drug dealers and all Native Americans were not drunks. I understood that all Jews were not occupiers and all Arabs were not terrorists. I was aware that all Asians were not mobsters. Even when stereotypes told me otherwise, I understood that every group had its own good, bad, and ugly.

Stereotypes are awfully economical with the truth and hopelessly illogical. They trade fact for personal agenda all the time. No one could correctly say that every member of his group was good and every member of another group was bad. Mischief is the stock of stereotypes in trade. Disaffection is what they peddle around. They specialize in weaving the errors of a few members of a group into huge baskets of generalizations. They oversimplify and make sweeping statements to make others look bad. Stereotypes lack the capacity to make balanced judgments. They are short of what it takes to walk as the crow flies. They need redirection before recognizing blue from red.

Maybe stereotypes should take a second look at themselves before making sweeping statements about other people.

Carl Jung suggested, "Everything that irritates us about others can lead us to an understanding of ourselves."

I strongly recommend that every group should think about this saying before judging others. People would discover that they were the reflections of what they thought about other people. You cannot look far from your neighborhood before finding the good and bad people you are looking for. Sometimes, they are right inside your household. Every group has its own shares of tall, short, slim, fat, sweet, obnoxious, faithful, atheistic, ethical, and perverted people.

I see your image when I look at the mirror. My image stares at you when you look at the mirror of judgment, Brother KKK. As I look at myself in the mirror, I see everything that I complain about you. When you look at yourself in the mirror, you will notice everything that you dislike about me. As I see criminals in your group, I see them in mine. As I see the racially prejudiced people in your group, I see them in mine. I ask that we should start seeing the good side of each other instead of the hideous side. Why does man like the bright side of the moon but prefer to see the dark side of fellow man? Man sets out at night to see the bright stars, but he favors seeing the dark side of mankind.

No culture is an island of angels. I see the good, bad, and ugly whenever I look at my neighborhood. I suppose that everyone who is willing to come out clean would agree with me. Every society has its finest and nastiest. I knew people who were good to a fault and people who were as bad as bad gets. There were generous as well as miserly people everywhere I lived. I was acquainted with some of the most straightforward people anywhere. I also knew some of the most corrupt ever. I had friends who were religious. Some did not profess any religion. I knew people who embraced diversity like the catechism of their existence. I knew those who did not see anything good in others. I was even familiar with people who shared affiliations with charitable organizations and those who belonged to dodgy gangs.

The world is filled with innumerable twists and tricky melodies. Only the wise can navigate the knotty routes of life. Only the shrewd can dance to its tunes. The wise does not judge the world in term of colors. They judge in terms of reality. There is no guarantee that everyone with your color would spare you. There is no proof that everyone who is different from you would kill you. Your perceived foe might shove you out of harm's way some day. Your assumed friend might dangle the legendary sword of Damocles around your neck some day. He who confides in people on the basis of their skin color would have his look-alikes remove his skin one day. I place my confidence in people on the basis of the contents of their characters, not the quantities of melanin in their skins.

Brother KKK, I know that your group has its own gifted as well as challenged people. You know that my group has its own shares of exceptional and ordinary people, too. My group could learn something from your group; your group could learn something from mine. How much do we learn from our right and left hands when they wash each other? The two hands can wash each other better and quicker than when one washes itself.

We both understand there are advanced and commonplace people in every group. It is difficult for one set to label another in disrespectful manners. Every group has a mastery of something. Knowing something more than another person does not call for labeling. That person may know something more than you. People have different gifts, just like nations have diverse endowments. Else, every country would have everything. There would be nothing called international trade and cooperation.

It is fine to feel good about oneself and what one knows. But it is best when done judiciously. Many do not have any problem with those who excel in given areas, but people frown at those who boast about themselves to irritate others. It is great to believe in one's heritage, but it should not be for the sole purpose of spiting others. Supporting one's people responsibly should make one a hero. But the hero becomes a villain when he starts hating on behalf of his people. Mankind could advance as an entity only when it adapts the diverse knowledge and energies for the common good of all and helps the challenged among us to reach their goals. The challenged are not necessarily who they are because they did not try. It could be because of factors beyond their control. It is easy to see other people's weaknesses because we are not in their shoes. Anyone who uses his strength or knowledge to spite the challenged is hopelessly weak and uninformed.

The world's apocalyptic clock is ticking toward midnight. Mankind must save itself from self-destruction. Superiority or inferiority will not matter if we allow the clock to proceed to the destructive end. All of mankind would be the loser. The labor of our ancestors and centuries of civilizations would be lost to man's idiocy. Both developed and developing worlds have ants up their sleeves. We must not give disintegration a chance. All nations, cultures, faiths, and groups have things to lose. Developed nations have civilizations to lose. Developing nations have dreams to lose. There could only be happiness in the presence of orderliness. He who promotes degeneration is mentally unwell, regardless of the side of the divide he belongs.

Brother KKK, we are dangling our common destiny by the sea cliff. We are holding our children's future to ransom as well. Man cannot nurture harmony and conflict simultaneously, just as he cannot cultivate civilization and terrorism in the same space of time. He cannot rear a rampaging bull in a china shop.

We have clear choices before us. Do we covet civilization or annihilation? Is man after harmony or conflict? Do we care about integration or disintegration? What do we want for our children when we are gone? How do we influence the coming generations' destinies when we are no longer here and cannot control the future again?

The future is in our hands now, Brother KKK. We cannot continue to poison our children's minds against one another. Let's stop our Napoleon before he reaches his Waterloo.

CHAPTER 5

▼

POISONED CHERUBS

No man has ever been born a Negro hater, a Jew hater, or any other kind of hater.
Nature refuses to be involved in such suicidal practices.
—Harry Bridges

Brother KKK, how fast time flies! We have not seen each other since we hugged in the street, moments after the aggressions against humanity on 9/11. I learned that your son, that is, my nephew, is growing so fast. I am pleased to inform you that my son, that is, your nephew, is growing swiftly. We are so blessed that our children will grow up and take over from where we left. They will cultivate the earth and raise their kinds. They will care and provide for their families. They will even leave the earth more beautiful for their own children. The beauty of the earth shall be our children's to behold. From Africa to the Middle East, Asia to Australia, Europe to Greenland, North America to the Pacific Islands, and South America to the Caribbean islands, man will be at peace with nature. Many generations of mankind would thrive and sustain the beautiful world.

The scenic plateaus, stunning waterfalls, and teeming game reserves of Africa will amaze our children. The abundance of grapes, olives, and cedar of the Middle East will astonish them. The magnificent mountains, icy slopes, and snaking rivers of Asia will bewitch them. Lily-filled fields, graciously rolling hills, and evergreen valleys of Europe will be gorgeous to our offspring. The imposing prairies, picturesque rocks, and awe-inspiring canyons of North America will be theirs. Our children will behold the beauties of the frothy oceans that straddle the continents. The heaving coastal mangroves, the breathtaking grasslands, the swarming forests, and the warm, sandy deserts of the world will belong to our young ones. The Statue of Liberty, Egyptian pyramids, Parthenon, Eiffel Tower, Coliseum of Rome, Great Wall of China, Taj Mahal, and relics of Mayan civilization will dazzle our progeny. They will be proud of their ancestors!

Wait a moment, Brother KKK. Did I say our children would be proud of their ancestors? Maybe it will not for everything that we pass on to them. Our progeny will be grateful for many things, but they will not be grateful for all. They will be thankful for the thriving cultures everywhere. They will be proud that we handed them the diverse techniques for tilling soil and raising livestock. They will be delighted that we taught them reading and writing, but they will not be delighted for transferring discrimination and chauvinism to them. Our children will be content that we transferred science and technology to them, but they will not be happy for teaching them how to judge and pull others down. They will be glad that we taught them calculus and logic, but they will not appreciate that we taught them to make stereotypes. They will not be proud if they hurt nature when fighting for flimsy reasons because we taught them warfare. Our children will not be pleased if the beautiful world suffers because they clashed over skin color, religions, and gangs. The young ones will not be proud that we taught them everything except how to get along.

Every generation is liable for transferring unhealthy biases to the one that comes after it. Our generation will be morally responsible if our children inherit discrimination, prejudice, and stereotypes from us. We will be guilty of manipulation if we influence our children to judge and hate, even when they were filled with love at birth. Our conscience will stand trial if our action leads the young ones to look down on others. Brother KKK, posterity would dock our scruples if our offspring detested those who are not like them.

What do we tell our children if they find out that hatred does not have any virtue? Can you imagine the infamy that would become our lot if our children look at us directly and ask, "Why did you mislead us?" Can we justify the vicious circle of hatred we are creating?

Every child is born pure. They do not know any difference between races and colors. They bear no grudges against others and do not underrate groups. Unless some people poison their little minds, the little cherubs remain adorable even as they turn into tots. It is unsettling how clean-minded toddlers absorb the prejudice that those before them pass on. Innocent children become accomplices in hate mongering. The blameless become the guilty party. The once-charming angels become poisoned cherubs that completely swallow the hatred learned from their elders. The greatest injustice that man could do for a child is teach him hatred when the latter arrives with his own agenda of affection for all. We manipulate children's minds and pass hatred to them as virtue. Man turns angels to demons, antidotes to venoms, and solutions to problems.

Clear as pure morning dew, children are the untainted, new members of mankind. They open their arms and embrace whoever embraces them. Unpolluted as the water fetched from the brook at dawn, infants are everyone's friends. They do not bear any grudges against races. They do not draw any lines between cultures. A child smiles at whoever smiles at him, regardless of the color of the friendly one. A child does not have any clue about religions until his surrounding world indoctrinates him. Youngsters enter into association with those who choose to be their friends, including their parents, family friends, peers, and responsive people from anywhere. Gangs mean nothing to a child until someone introduces him to one. Obviously, every generation is liable for transferring evil to the one after it.

I have a story to prove my innocence before the ones before me weighed me into their world. I bet that you, Brother KKK, have a story to confirm your transparency before the adult members of your group engulfed you with their belief. We were not haters until the generation before us raped our conscience. Instead of coercing us to uphold their judgments, I wished the elders allowed us to explore, observe, and make our own judgments about other cultures. Rather than ramming their condemnatory views down our innocent throats, I hoped they had allowed us to make our own meanings out of the puzzling world. I wished the seniors did not make us the zombies who did their biddings. They did not even give us a chance to give the world a taste of our innocence.

This is my story, my chronicle. This was my world as an adorable cherub. This was the part of me that puts the ones before me to trial. I will give you the account of what convicts my elders. When I was a toddler, I welcomed everyone into my world. I opened the door of my heart widely for all who smiled at me as a child. There were no bars of color in my world. I had no idea that there were races. The varied skin colors looked beautiful to me. Diverse religions seemed like assorted ways of worshiping the only God. Rather than skin color, I cherished smiling faces that came with acts of kindness. I welcomed beaming and smirking mouths that spoke unfamiliar languages, but I despised frowning mouths that uttered mean words in my language. The world was beautiful and pure to me. As I kept growing, every day was a new day for unearthing something new.

I believed in one world with one destiny and one God. All men looked the same to me, regardless of their nationalities and mother tongues. I was so innocent. I even assumed that the world started and ended in the small town where I was born. I did not have any idea there was another world elsewhere. My town appeared like the only municipality, realm, and sphere. It was the lone world that existed. I went to church with my family on Sunday, but I played with my friends that embraced other faiths. I was not afraid of my Muslim friends. They were not scared of me either. I did not have any adversaries. I supposed there was one indivisible God with no languages too many to worship. So many in diverse ways and languages put him on a pedestal. Life seemed so good. Serenity was all that humanity cared about. The world around me was at peace with itself. I could not have been happier. Nature thrived in beauty everywhere. My little town seemed like the center of the world and the only earth. I was a happy little boy who had the whole world as his friends.

I had the freedom to reason on my own except when my elders were telling me new things. I explored on my own before the seniors started teaching me different things about the world. One beautiful morning, I even snuck out of sight when the elders thought I could gaze at the skies by myself outside the house. I witnessed the gorgeous sun inching its way up the eastern horizon. The unbelievable glory appeared to be rising from the ground and climbing up the sky. The huge sun appeared smaller as it climbed farther into the sky. I looked as far as my eyes could see. It seemed like the heavens enveloped my little town. It appeared like the sky touched the ground some distance away.

"There is no harm in walking the distance and touching the sky where it meets the ground," I thought. "It would be amazing to see the hole from which the sun emerged a while ago before climbing into the skies."

Thus, I began my first exploration of the wide, wild world. Interestingly, the closer I thought I was to the place where the ground met the sky, the farther the sky moved away from me. The farther I hiked toward the rim of the sky, the farther it became. Soon, I got lost at some part of the town that I had not visited. The more I tried to figure out my way, the more I seemed lost. I stood at a street corner somewhere and cried, searching for attention from whoever cared to assist a crying little boy. A relative happened to be at the right place at the right time. She recognized me instantly and took me safely to my grandmother's home. Nobody hurt me. The world was harmless and innocent back then. Imagine the chaste power of innocence in a child! That was the story of an innocent child who deserved to live in an innocent world.

Did you ask for my story's bottom line, Brother KKK? I was an innocent child. The adults could have allowed me to retain my innocent agenda of love for all. I could have held onto my thought that all men were the same and skin colors were mere varieties. I could have retained my religion, but remained tolerant of other faiths. I could have seen associations that people joined for the common good of all, not for the selfish and wicked interest of a few. Regrettably, the elders turned me to a panel that they could shape with their judgmental mallets. I was grateful that they told me about the existence of other towns, nations, continents, and even planets besides the little town I knew. I was glad they acquainted me with a diverse world with assorted cultures. Unfortunately, they went beyond the curriculum and told me uncomplimentary stories about other cultures, faiths, and beliefs.

The adults placed unnecessary emphasis on races and skin colors. It was more than I needed to know or willing to stomach. They made some groups look better than others. They even called some evil. They instructed me that some cultures were fine and some were appalling. They could have said there were good and bad people in every culture. A perception was born. I began to look at the world in terms of good and bad cultures instead of good and bad individuals. I lost my perspective for looking at the world. I began to look at mankind with the biased view of the elders. My views of the world became blurred as I tried to see through the seniors' prism of prejudice.

"Maybe the elders were right and I was wrong," I thought, struggling with the idea repeatedly.

Thank goodness for nature's gift of independent reasoning to every man who chooses to think on his own without subjecting his interpretation to the prejudiced minds of others. There comes a time when a boy becomes a man and conscience holds him accountable for his actions without giving him room for explaining how society influenced him. As I matured, I had a renaissance of tolerance. My conscience started to hold me accountable for my beliefs, not what some seniors in my community made me believe about the world. The turning point was complete as I began to appreciate realism in place of the radicalism that the elders passed down. The time was right to fashion my own identity and stand up for my own beliefs, just like everyone stands accountable for his actions.

Every man stands up for his belief, but the contents of a man's belief determine if other men would stand up for him. I knew a man could believe in whatever he wanted. But did his beliefs make fellow men respect him? I understood that prejudice was no longer fashionable and bigotry continued to belittle men and women who embraced it. Clearly, the world honored men and women who used their influences to advance human causes, not those who tried to subdue mankind in anarchy. I understood why the world defeated Adolf Hitler and celebrated Martin Luther King Jr. instead. I could identify with how the world relegated Idi Amin Dada and elevated Nelson Mandela. I knew why the world celebrated Mahatma Gandhi and rejected Slobodan Milosevic. It was no longer a secret to me why some men had generous places in history and others had their names constricted to the footnotes of history.

I chose to stand by what my conscience dictated and not what others said. I wanted to be a leader with mission and vision, not a blind follower. Leaders are the true masters of their fates, but sightless followers determine their uncertain fates. The man who swallows what another man says completely without processing it in his head remains inferior in his body, soul, and spirit forever. I respected my elders' opinions, but I understood I would be accountable for my own belief, not my elders' conviction. The advice of elders benefits youths. But, when the youths become adults, it is advisable for the youths to double-check that they received real advice. I did not mind standing by what my friends said, but they were not right all the time. Real men do not follow their friends because they were friends. They follow their friends because they were right.

Brother KKK, you and I have two things to worry about. History will hold us answerable for them. We are responsible for the choices we make as adults. We are accountable for what we pass on to the innocent, younger generations. Our elders were liable for the prejudice they passed to us as naïve children, but we are responsible for our beliefs when we become adults and fail to reprocess what we heard from the elders. An irresponsible person holds others responsible for his beliefs because he failed to use his own brain. Instead, he allowed others to do his thinking for him. Any man who transferred to his children all that his parents told him, without weighing them, did not realize that his parents were not perfect.

The men who accept the evils that their ancestors passed down never grow up to become men of their own. They remain inseparable from the malevolent aprons that their fathers owned. They would drag their own children through the dark alley of impiety against their will. Women who accept the wicked advice of their predecessors will remain as their mothers' poodles. The youths who fail to reprocess what they learned from their elders will become liable for nursing wickedness all the days of their lives. I embraced compassion after I reprocessed the anger that some of my elders passed down. Clemency overtook my heart after the reprocessing of the harshness I got from some relatives. I approved of the liberation from hatred that my heart now enjoys.

Benevolent traditions are worth transferring to one's children, but inhumane practices are not worth reassigning, even to one's enemy. The good deeds we pass to our offspring will yield good seeds, but the appalling acts we reassign to our enemies will return to our children because what goes around comes around. The best favor a man could do for himself is to spread charity. He will never have reasons to fear that what goes around will come back as evil. Every good man understands that good deeds generate good seeds. However, hateful conducts yield evil products. Therefore, I will transfer love to my children. Not only will hatred hurt others, the vicious circle without any final place of rest might come back to my offspring vehemently.

Hatred is evil. Nobody embraces evil except the evil. The evil man thinks, speaks, hears, sees, dreams, does, and encourages evil. Prejudice is wicked. No one appreciates wickedness except the wicked. The wicked woman bears, delivers, nurtures, supports, teaches, cheers, and spreads wickedness. Hatred and prejudice will not find their ways from me to my children, just like evil and wickedness will not find a place in my abode. I will not think of, speak of, hear, see, dream, do, and encourage evil. Thus, my offspring will not bear, deliver, nurture, support, teach, cheer, and spread wickedness.

Brother KKK, the sage warned that the evils that men do live after them. Unfortunately, evil men lack the power to stop the evil they left behind from haunting their children thereafter. Those who engage in acts of benevolence have nothing to lose. The goodwill they leave behind has the audacity of sending random showers of blessings their children's way. I do not make any pacts with evil, so nothing will separate my children from goodness when I am gone from the surface of the earth. It is my desire and pleasure to live more than an arm's length away from evil, so wickedness will not become my children's neighbor. My actions will generate nothing except goodness and mercy for my offspring as they tread the frail roads of life.

The wise embrace pragmatism; the fool cuddles impracticality. Who else besides the confused give away the truth in pursuit of deceit? Wise men stand by profitable ideals; foolish men stand by non-lucrative principles that ego initiates. Progressive people light the world for all to see; warped people obstruct the light so others might misstep and fall. Shrewd minds spread charity across the board. They understand that what goes around comes around. Bewildered minds spread hatred elsewhere because they assume that what happens elsewhere stays elsewhere. They forget that mankind dwells in one world that is devoid of cast-iron borders. We share the same oceans. The skies lack filters across nations. Currents move the same waters from one continent to another. The ever-flowing atmosphere transfers air from one land to another. Surely, what goes around will come around some day.

Brother KKK, those who hate understand little about the amount of energy they dissipate for nothing. They know little about the quantity of vigor they squander on unprofitable endeavors. Haters could not figure out that the evil they expect the ocean to carry to other lands will find its way back to shore some day. Tides and time will bring back the charity that men send abroad, just like currents and events will return the evil that men send across the ocean. Man will eventually breathe the dust he generated into passing wind when air currents will change direction and return to where it started. He who lives to make the world a better place should not stop. He who does evil should beware. Good and bad have relevant consequences.

Time is not as long as a street. Life is not as elongated as a rope. Men sometimes, somewhere, and somehow wish they could have done something differently, but time seldom permits evil men to right all of the wrongs they invested in life. History will be fair to those who leave life better than they found it. Mean accounts will trail those who invest nothing except evil in life. Every man who seeds gratifying moisture into the air leaves showers of blessings for his children. The man who blows harsh air into the sky leaves nothing except cruel baths for his offspring. Whatsoever a man disseminates, his children will garner. Does any man still doubt that the evil he does live after him?

This is my recommendation, Brother KKK. Sow whatever seed you want to sow in life today. Do not wait for tomorrow. Tomorrow may never come. Today is here for you to spend as you wish. Whatever you do, Brother KKK, do not teach children how to hate. Children come into the world with all of the innocence available in the heaven. They have an agenda of love for all. Robbing children of their innocence and the agenda of love is a foremost transgression against humanity. Crimes are an affront against fellow men. They have their terms of sentences. But it is only men without conscience, nature's great gift to mankind, that rob children of their hearts of gold. Any man who teaches children how to hate will show them the path to historical perdition.

No individuals, nations, or cultures that hated others in history earned the world's respect. They isolated themselves from the comity of people with conscience until they said good-bye to hatred and welcomed love for all. Their names were missing from the halls of fame everywhere until they said goodnight to abhorrence and good morning to affection for mankind. There is redemption for haters who turn their lives around, but there is no grace for those who embrace hatred without remorse. Hatred has no virtue. Whatever lacks virtue cannot be good. Whatever is not good cannot be right. You cannot be right and be wrong. Whatever has no virtue cannot be right. He who hates shall remain a burden to himself and his kind until he embraces charity.

Children raised in hateful environments have the unfortunate luck of bearing the burden of hatred as long as they live to hate. Children raised in charitable environments have access to blissful living as long as they embrace benevolence instead of malevolence. Haters have limited friends. They inhabit a little world without any room for charity. Those who love have countless friends and live in a boundless world that is large enough for all to get along happily. The fear of sharing blinds those who hate. They cannot see the countless and boundless opportunities abounding in a united world. How much love does a hater have for his own people when he lacks affection and his heart lacks room for charity?

Brother KKK, it is time for our generation to return the love we stole from the younger generations. We must give back the charity that we denied our children. The youths need to hear new stories about other people. Our generation must sing a new song that lacks discordant lyrics containing woes about others. The stolen hearts of gold should return to the rightful owners, the young and innocent ones. The fact that our ancestors robbed us of love for all does not justify our desire to transfer hatred to our own children. The vicious circle of abhorrence should end. There is no civilization if mankind has yet to refrain from the archaic ways of treating one another. Our generation has the moral responsibility to end the charade we transferred to the younger generations.

We cannot look at our children directly and say we did not rob the innocence that nature bestowed on them. We robbed the innocent hearts of gold and rubbed salt on the injury scarred on them. We stole the young people's innocence in exchange for our incensed code of hatred, just like our elders did. The vicious circle of hatred now has a free reign because we did not make any efforts to break the jinx. How dare you and I sustain the principle that lacks virtue? Why did we pass on the lackluster standard of odium? Why do we labor in vain to sustain that which breeds enemies but not friends? Hatred does not bring any friends and does not breed any goodwill for its owner. He who hates reaps nothing except broken hearts as long as he lives. His heart bleeds as he watches those he hates thrive. Our children do not deserve broken hearts for all the days of their lives.

My heart bleeds for your son, that is, my nephew, and my son, that is, your nephew. They are the innocent sufferers of our many wars of attrition. Remember that the grass suffers when two elephants clash. The innocent suffers when giants fight, just like ordinary people breathe the dust when gladiators clash.

Brother KKK, what did our innocent children do to deserve bearing the substantial, but bleak, burden of hatred we bestowed on them? Can't we just spare them the pains of joining the fray?

They must be relieved of the hopeless burden of revulsion before we could get a reprieve from posterity. The young cherubs gave their clean hearts to the world before we forced them to bear the fangs of hatred.

Let's trim the fangs of hatred. They know not who to bite, what to bite, when to bite, why they bite, and how to bite decently. The vicious teeth of hatred bite everyone, including those who bear them. They gnaw those they should not and nibble when they should not. The cruel teeth of hatred do not have any clue why they chew and do not know how to bite without spilling blood. Our children, the little angels, must not bear the spiteful fangs of hatred. They came into the world with gentle gums of love, not teeth. Nature would not forgive us. Posterity would hold us accountable if we fail to spare the cherubs from drinking the wine of prejudice that our generation brewed. Bad parents teach kids about dominant and remnant cultures in a world that yearns for equality.

▼

CHAPTER 6

DOMINANT PARADIGM

Before God we are all equally wise—and equally foolish ... Whoever undertakes to set himself up as a judge of Truth and Knowledge is shipwrecked by the laughter of the gods.
—Albert Einstein

Brother KKK, what can we learn from the lower animals? Why does man pride himself with superiority when he also lives in the "dog eats dog" world? Despite our knowledge, we rarely treat one another better than how the lower animals treat each other. Obviously, man is ahead in science and technology. Our incursion into space and ability to manipulate the environment make us special. But the lower animals are social and creative in their own ways. Except when we invade and manipulate their habitats, they survive in their communities. They are knowledgeable about many things. Beavers build their own dams. Birds construct their nests. Squirrels burrow their tunnels. I marvel at how land and sea animals understand the seasons and migrate over long distances on their own.

Man manipulates the environment to get what he wants, but lower animals depend solely on their natural abilities. It stuns me how lesser animals sense forthcoming tsunamis unaided and move to higher grounds before water arrives when man, except with the aid of one of his many contraptions, could not. It amazes me how dogs sniff out the most hideous dangers, but man could not do the same without pieces of equipment. Dogs are loyal to friends and often protective of their own, regardless of their colors or breeds. Brother KKK, I could imagine you thinking about what happens to the "dog eats dog" theme if dogs were nice to one another. Man coined "dog eats dog" to explain how man manipulates other men in the struggle for survival. Any human who anoints himself as the judge of truth and knowledge over others has not learned how to respect and get along with fellow men. Certainly, man has to humble himself and learn something from lower animals.

Ironically, despite his knowledge, man has yet to figure out how to get along with fellow men. Lower animals do not fight simply because they hate each other, but man does. Lower animals do not clash as a result of prejudice against one another, but man does. Lesser animals do not despise each other because of discrimination and they do not engage in stereotypes, but man does. Lower animals do what they do instinctively, and this is not because they are mischievous. But man, who should know better, has a hard time engaging his knowledge to place prejudice, discrimination, stereotypes, and repression where they belonged. Man expends knowledge for annihilating, demeaning, detesting, thwarting, and yoking other men. He who lacks knowledge is ignorant, but he who hurts others with knowledge is ignorant.

Elvis Presley said, "Animals don't hate, and we're supposed to be better than them."

Prejudice has its roots in one man's perception that he is better than another man. Claiming to be superior and more knowledgeable than others in an endless universe of diverse knowledge is simply naïve. It is like the inexperienced who said that his father's farm was larger than the farms of other people's fathers' when he knew little about other people's farms. Knowledge is relative and too diverse to quantify. Excelling in certain aspects of knowledge should not make a man look down on others.

Why does man burden himself with being the master of knowledge when knowledge is unconquerable in its entirety? The claim of superiority by one man over another reveals man's fascination by ego, not knowledge itself. Real knowledge is devoid of mischief and arrogance.

The truly knowledgeable person is capable of differentiating good from evil. He does not engage knowledge for depraved, supercilious, and deceitful purposes. He does not take advantage of others or disrespects fellow humans. Knowledge becomes malice when it reeks of unwarranted pride and ego. It turns evil when it takes advantage of others. A knowledgeable person recognizes what he knows and acknowledges what others have. The man who claims to be knowledgeable but disrespects what other people know is grossly uninformed. Understanding and courtesy are major parts of knowledge. Knowledge is not evil unless it comes with a sense of self and brings others down. Real knowledge does not minimize others and distances itself from ego.

Knowledge is wisdom; wisdom means understanding. Understanding connotes selflessness, thoughtfulness, acceptance, consideration, appreciation, and kindness. Whoever claims to be knowledgeable but is deficit in understanding lacks wisdom.

Jean-Jacques Rousseau, the famous French philosopher, had the same opinion. He asked, "What wisdom can you find that is greater than kindness?"

Knowledge is a gift of nature for the benefit of mankind. It is the light for guiding man's feet. No man puts on light and hides it. The bearer of light is the custodian, and he is not the only one who is intended to see with the light. Like candlelight, knowledge is not enduring when flaunted arrogantly in the wind. Knowledge is beautiful, meaningful, moderate, considerate, and thoughtful. It is not hurtful. The enlightened man who hurts people with his light is not a light-bearer. He bears fire and burns others. The light-bearer cannot be arrogant. Else, his light would turn a conflagration that burns people's feet instead of guiding them.

Knowledge is unlimited. Man should not despise others when knowledge reveals itself. Imagine how shameful it is if the culture that discovered metal had claimed superiority forever, oblivious of the fact that another culture would discover silicon chips in the future.

Never ever say never. We cannot definitely say which culture would discover what in a thousand years. But that is saying that mankind is still here. What if Rome had claimed to be the last empire standing? I modestly submit that the truly knowledgeable man understands how little he knows and how frail his seemingly vast understanding is within an endless cosmos of knowledge. Man creates problems when he assumes that he knows it all. An instance is when man generates anarchy with faith, that is, a fundamental part of knowledge, by flaunting his religion in other people's faces. Being considerate, loving, caring, forgiving, and praying for others are better ways of showcasing faith.

Brother KKK, I was humbled the day I learned a lesson about knowledge and superiority. I realized that one should not look down on others because of his assumed level of knowledge and understanding. It started with a young man who acquired knowledge and tried to flaunt it. I returned to the village with a lot of accomplishments and pride as a fresh college graduate. Pleased with how much I knew about geography, economics, mathematics, sciences, languages, logic, and philosophy.

I explained to an elderly neighbor why he should send his children to school. Almost prophetically, I suggested, "They'll be better off if they go to school."

I did not start out to hurt the man's feelings, but he looked at me suspiciously, smiled, and asked, "What do you mean by sending my children to school?"

I did not have an answer for a moment because I thought my proposal was self-explicit enough for anyone to comprehend.

"Knowledge is power after all," I thought.

I was not sure if the man truly understood me or he was just trying to be mischievous. He just smiled and looked suspiciously at me. The more I looked at him, his frozen smile puzzled me more. I was not sure if I were to be amused or prepare myself for a long debate of wits. The man grinned at me apprehensively as he nodded. That kind of grinning seemed to make the other man appear stupid, but I stood my grounds.

"I meant your children would be better in life if they go to school," I explained, rephrasing what I said earlier.

The man did not appear either pleased or irritated when I meddled in his family's affairs. I thought that everyone should share in my newly found life of education that heralded enlightenment and success. I was convinced that I was right. I did not expect anyone to be offended when I tried to encourage other members of the community to become knowledgeable.

"Does my proposition offend you?" I asked innocently.

"Offended? No! We are just trying to learn something from one another," he said. He was still smiling, but he was looking at me apprehensively. He looked at me and asked, "Do you truly think that my children are not knowledgeable?"

Then he explained a lot of things that I took for granted.

"My children might not have been to the university like you, but they are well-schooled in what they do," he said confidently.

Like him, his children were farmers. His explanation made me remember something that I read from a book years earlier. Now it made more sense to me than when I first read it. "My children have firsthand encounters with the soils, instead of reading about them in books. They are well acquainted with the different seasons. They know the names of the trees and animals in this region. They recognize the crops that thrive in the different soils and the amounts of water they need. They are familiar with the pests that distress each crop as well as the right time to sow and harvest the diverse crops." The man explained that his children probably understood the soils more than me.

Brother KKK, it appeared like my neighbor was educating me when I thought I knew everything he did not know. "My children understand the many sounds of the animals and what they mean. They know the clouds that bring rains and the ones that have nothing to offer except howling winds. They spend their spare time weaving some of the most artistic clothing materials and baskets whenever they have little to do at the farm. People even come from the university to look at what my children make. They often buy them to show the other members of the university," bragged the man.

"My children couldn't have been lacking in knowledge if people from the university pay for what they make so educated people could learn from them," stated the man, still smiling at me.

"I didn't mean that your children lacked knowledge," I said defensively.

Knowledge has a way of making the offensive to become defensive when it encounters a different sort of knowledge. I realized we could learn from each other if we were patient and respected one another. I tried to bring the discussion to perspective. I did not start out to offend the man and his family. I tried to make them see the good side of education. I was not trying to disrespect their subsistence style of living. I wanted them to improve on what they knew how to do. I thought I should respect the man's perspective. What he said made a lot of sense to me. I was beginning to learn something from his side of the story. My neighbor succeeded in getting me to understand that knowledge is relative after all. It does not end with the ability to fabricate weapons of mass destruction.

"Education improves people's lives in many ways. It widens people's horizons," I explained to the man as he continued to stare at me.

The small talk was no longer a debate between an educated man and an illiterate. It was a contest between someone who acquired knowledge through school and the other who gained knowledge from experience. I could not contest what my neighbor was saying. He was making sense. The only thing that separated his children from me was that I learned at an organized school and they had learned from experience. His children knew some things better than me, despite my modern education. I could match only a few of the many trees in that part of the world with their names. I only recognized some of the sounds that the different animals made. I knew little about what they meant. But the man's children knew those better.

"What do you think about the childless counselor, fresh from school, who tries to advise an illiterate mother of eight on parenting?" demanded the man, sounding like a sarcastic college professor. "The all-knowing, educated youth should ask the illiterate mother how she raised the seven grown-up kids before teaching her how to nurture the infant eighth," advised the man tenaciously. "What people read in books requires some practicality when it comes to real life."

Then he nodded. But I started thinking. Those who knew so much about the seasons, soils, animals, and crafts should know something instinctively about sciences, mathematics, logic, and arts.

The Pharaohs' draftsmen were not versed in modern architecture. But they built the most magnificent pyramids. They did not attend contemporary, prestigious universities, but they built the spectacular Sphinx that puzzles modern designers. The Mayan builders did not learn up-to-date urban planning, but their cities make modern planners jealous. The ancient Greeks constructed an astounding acropolis without attending modern colleges. The builder of the Taj Mahal probably did not go to college. Consider the people of Mesopotamia, the culture that tamed the Euphrates and Tigris to support a remarkable civilization. They did not attend modern colleges. There are no records to show that those who erected Stonehenge studied architecture at a university either.

"I appreciate educated people and learn from them a lot. But can you say with all certainty that people like me lack knowledge, even when university people learn from our works?" asked the man resolutely.

I still wanted to emphasize the importance of education, but I could not disagree with his reasoning. Organized knowledge had its roots in the natural environment. Arguably, one could not describe those who learned from the natural environment as lacking in knowledge just because they did not go to organized schools. I decided to humble myself and listen to more of the man's story. I could not deny the fact that I was learning something fresh from him. I guessed he was learning something useful from me as well.

Brother KKK, I wish you witnessed the ideological exchange between my elderly neighbor and me. I defined knowledge from my own perspective. He characterized it from his own angle. I was sure of my position, but I could not fault his position either. I began to see the different faces of knowledge and diverse phases of education. I thought about the fact that people eat dinner everywhere. The difference lies in the diverse dishes and the different times they serve them. I associated what transpired between my elderly neighbor and me with the world. I could not agree more with the fact that every culture has unique knowledge and mankind would benefit if we would harmonize the diverse knowledge. I could imagine the benefits of learning from one another instead of engaging in wars of attrition over whose knowledge is superior.

Albert Einstein, the celebrated icon of knowledge of his time, does not need any introduction. He knew exactly what he was promoting when he explained that all men were uniformly shrewd and evenly irrational before God. The father of atomic physics also had his reasons for maintaining that the laughter of the gods would ground the vessel of whoever assigned himself the role of arbitrator of truth and knowledge. I think my neighbor and I were uniformly shrewd and evenly irrational before the deity. The gods must have laughed their heads off as I inadvertently set my education above my neighbor's knowledge. I was glad that I acted like an unassuming man early enough. It was better than becoming a humbled man in the face of my old neighbor's time-tested knowledge.

My neighbor congratulated me for my newly acquired degree and revealed something interesting about himself. "I appreciate organized education so much and sometimes lament that something is missing in my life," he conceded. I was glad that he admitted that something was missing in his life. "My children would get more education as soon as they could. I agree that educated people have more options and better opportunities to advance in life," he said.

It was pleasing that the man appreciated education after all. However, I could not deny the fact that he was very knowledgeable in the absence of my type of education. I observed that he was enjoying the debate between a young graduate from an organized school and an elderly farmer from the school of life. That was after he observed that I was willing to listen to his own point of view.

Brother KKK, my neighbor and I were now having fun, exchanging ideas about knowledge. It appeared no one had any hard feelings toward the other beside the new line of discussion and camaraderie.

"I respect your type of knowledge, but I'm sometimes concerned about the problems associated with it," affirmed the neighbor.

I could not comprehend his latest assertion, and I did not pretend to understand him either. "Why are you concerned about the type of knowledge that improves people's lives significantly?" I asked rather suspiciously.

The man tried to explain what he meant. He said, "Knowledge is supposed to improve people's lives, but it sometimes offers challenges to mankind. I appreciate knowledge, but I frown at how it opens the door for those who hurt mankind."

The ominous look on his face was unmistakable. He said, "I welcome the branches of knowledge for healing and doing other good things, not the ones for massive killing and other evils. People like me don't have the type of knowledge for killing masses of people within minutes."

I could not prove the man wrong yet. Some educated people misuse the knowledge meant for making life better. They create weapons of mass destruction with the same knowledge needed for generating electricity and other comforts. Educated people, not peasants, were responsible for Agent Orange, sarin, mustard, and other nerve agents for annihilating multitudes of humans. The old man made me think.

"It appears like some clever people don't know the essence of knowledge. The more knowledge they discover, the more problems they create for mankind," he argued. "Peasants do not depreciate the environment as educated industrialists do. The big businesses that run the environment down are educated people's babies."

"Educated people polarize the world with their knowledge, but subsistence farmers, like me, use their knowledge for sustaining people. They talk about ordinary people only when there is something in it for them, but they dump us when they don't need us. How fair are the educated people?"

He knew what he was talking about, and he had good examples to support his arguments, too. It was very educative listening to the old fox.

"Life shouldn't be as decadent as educated people are making it. Immoralities and indiscipline are growing because of uncontrolled civilization. Educated people are drunk with unrestrained civilization, and they are turning away from realities," he added, now somber.

"It's ironic that education, which was meant to make man know better, has turned him into a zombie," he said solemnly.

"I knew my right from wrong early enough. My parents disciplined me, but educated people now call it abuse when loving parents try to discipline their own children. Educated people are condemning everything done by our parents to make us great citizens. Our children are now becoming self-centered in our very eyes!"

The man said, "The more educated people try to prove that there is no God, the more perverted mankind becomes. Sellers signified the prices of those goods with the number of rocks left next to them. Buyers left the same amounts of money when they purchased them. Nobody stole anything. All believed that someone was watching them from above. Educated people now explain why perversion is rampant in society, except that God is missing in their explanations."

"Previous generations covered their bodies because they understood it was immoral to do otherwise. But civilization now dictates that humans have to reveal the hallowed parts of their bodies to look good," he lamented. "People now base their lives on what studies say, not what common sense dictates. The same people behind studies that say coffee is good for one's health today might say it is bad for the body tomorrow."

I could sense the distress in the man's voice more than ever.

"How superior is the uncertain knowledge that takes people back and forth? How advanced is the civilization that awards medals to men and women that divorce spouses most?" he asked with a tinge of regret. "I did not go to school, but I understand it is immoral to expose certain parts of the body. I know that failing to spank a wayward child would not make him any better."

I could understand my neighbor's concerns. It was not unusual to hear earful talks like that on daily basis. I knew things were going out of control and people were swaying back and forth under the currents that advancement generated.

"Civilization is like a circle. People start from one point and return to the same crude beginning if they don't know where to stop. It's like the clock that moves from one to twelve and ends up going back to one," I said, showing solidarity to my neighbor, hoping the sparkle could return to his face.

The man became radiant momentarily, just like someone who just received an answer to his prayer for support. I could not fault the knowledge lurking inside his brain.

Who wouldn't be interested in what the man had to say next? It seemed like a philosophy class where students and a lecturer challenged one another to bouts of game of reasoning. My neighbor was undoubtedly a philosopher in his own right. He had demonstrated how educated people, who should know better, sometimes failed mankind. He now wanted to show how educated people had more worries than ordinary people. The man pointed at a group of peasants playing a game nearby.

"Can you see how happy they look, despite living simple lives?" asked the man almost suspiciously.

Truly, the people were laughing heartily as they placed the seeds into the holes on the wooden board while savoring the traditional game.

"They may not be as educated as you, but they have fewer things to worry about," explained the man.

I was uncomfortable with my neighbor's new picture of knowledge. I thought we should get to the bottom of his differences with edification.

He tried to explain why he felt that peasants, compared to educated people, had little to worry about. He pointed at the airplane that was cruising at thousands of feet above us.

"God forbid, I'm not trying to be mean, but peasants are not scared that one might fall to the ground. I've not boarded one. I don't intend to be on one ever," suggested the man regrettably.

"People sometimes die on the ground when airplanes crash on them," I reminded the old man, but he did not flinch.

"You are educated. Do the math. Compared to the passengers of crashed airplanes, how many people have died on the ground?" he asked, just like a convinced professor. "I could say that ordinary people take life easy. We go one day at a time. Educated people die of heart attacks over little things." The old man was sure of what he was talking about.

"For the most part, I eat unsullied fruits and vegetables from my farm. I cook fresh animals from the farm, but people like you eat refrigerated foods most of the time," he asserted.

I could not contest what he was saying. I had eaten a frozen meal minutes before my encounter with him. However, I did not want to become a willing conspirator against knowledge.

"I guess you are not against knowledge. You are against the part of knowledge that hurts people," I suggested.

My old neighbor clarified once again that he admired knowledge. "I respect knowledgeable people. I cannot stand those who hate education, but I despise those who use knowledge for hurting people and those who hide behind civilization to ruin young people," he emphasized.

A little over two decades after my encounter with him, my old neighbor's grievances are now clearer. Warring nations and terrorists are now taking advantage of the knowledge meant for good things. They are engaging knowledge for killing, maiming, and ruining lives around the world.

"Knowledge is not superior when it has the ability to nullify peace. It is compelling only when it does not erase its potency," said the old man when I thought he was done. "Mankind was given knowledge so he could live above the challenges of his environment, but man ended up nullifying good knowledge by using it for evil."

I had never seen any of the people that I once thought to be uninformed come that far.

"I dare knowledgeable people to channel all of their knowledge into causes that benefit mankind. Otherwise, knowledge would not be superior and surpass ignorance. It would remain just an instrument of evil," he concluded.

Some people from the university were waiting for him. They wanted to find out how he managed to have a bumper harvest while the university's demonstration farm had a poor one.

"Phew!" I whistled as the man walked away.

I understood his worries about knowledge and mankind. People tout themselves or their groups as superior to others. However, the encounter with my old neighbor provided an insight into how hollow those superiority arguments sounded. A man's wealth cannot be a good measure of how happy he is. Excelling in certain aspects of knowledge should not be a good reason for looking down on others, who possibly excel in other areas. Self-accolades by conceited individuals usually prevent them from recognizing other people's successes.

Albert Einstein said, "Before God, we are all equally wise and equally foolish … Whoever undertakes to set himself up as a judge of truth and knowledge is shipwrecked by the laughter of the gods."

Who among us would disagree with this?

CHAPTER 7

▼

COMMON GROUNDS

If we were to wake up some morning and find that everyone was the same race, creed and color, we would find some other cause for prejudice by noon.
—George Aiken

Brother KKK, I should inform you that I woke up this morning with the wisdom of an oracle. The seer gave me a prophecy. He said that nature, in its colossal wisdom, created the world magnificently so one part could complement and compliment the other. Nonetheless, man, in his infinitesimal wisdom, was looking for the superior and inferior parts of nature. We engage chauvinism as a tool for tearing apart the grand work of nature. Mankind grants prejudice the permission to rule when it should be a voiceless, shapeless, and powerless nonentity. Intolerance exists at our mercy because we tolerate it. We lost control the day we allowed prejudice, a diminutive scheme, to define itself as a giant. We could minimize prejudice if we diminish it, and it might as well become an idol if we venerate it. We should place prejudice where it belongs. Else, it would place us where we do not belong.

Prejudice is getting more attention because man is misusing common grounds. We seek common grounds mischievously by identifying with those who look like us, but we exclude others. Don't misunderstand it now. Common ground is natural. It is a good idea, but the concept does not know where to stop once we grant it free right of passage. One could explain the idea exceptionally well with the political paradigm we have today. The West has the common ground of being the well-off nations, but we exclude developing nations. The developing world has its own common grounds to counter the developed world's common grounds. Then common grounds keep going down the chain because they do not know where to stop. Unconsciously, mankind allows common grounds to transcend common growth. We continue to generate wedges between ourselves.

Man continues to crave common grounds with people who have things in common with him, but he excludes people who look different. The developed world forms smaller political, economic, and power blocks when the bigger group bores it. The European, North American, and Asian blocks go their own ways when the bigger common ground can no longer satisfy their specific interests. The smaller political blocks do not remain permanent either. Nations keep dividing into smaller groups, seeking further common grounds. The United States, for instance, distinguishes herself into a national unit when she has a reason to do so. Interestingly, prosperity, political stability, and military might appear not appealing enough to stop American citizens from pursuing further common grounds as a single group. Common grounds further separate Americans into whites, blacks, Hispanics, Asians, Native Americans, Alaskans, or Pacific Islanders.

Always seeking common grounds, people move down to the regional level to form bonds with those who live in the same regions with them. However, they exclude those who reside in other regions, regardless of whether they belonged to the same race, religion, or group. In the United States, residents of the Northeast talk about the desert dwellers in the Southwest when seeking common grounds with other people in the Northeast. Southwest inhabitants talk about the freezer dwellers that live in the Northeast in winter. People come together when they feel threatened collectively, but they recoil into their individual tents when they feel better. How, when, where, what, and who would tame common grounds?

Living in the same city does not stop people from seeking common grounds down the chain. They create social boundaries around the city on the basis of race, economic strength, faith, class, and gangs. Males form common grounds with fellow males, but they exclude females. They even initiate boys into thinking about what bonds them with men. Once again, they exclude the girls.

"Boys would be boys," they say.

Grown females form their own alliance and carry the girls with them, but they exclude the males. Man is yet to tame the common ground monster that divides people at will. Common grounds continue to separate mankind down the line.

Some even carry common grounds too far. They establish bonds with some of their children, but they exclude others. Common grounds become "divide and rule" and a nightmare when man bears it too far. It happens among friends, at places of work, among groups, government officials, and everywhere. Common grounds should not be bad things, but we carry them too far often. It is human nature to seek common grounds. Yet, like freedom, food, water, air, and other good things of life, common grounds become poisonous when they bear their fangs. It is okay to share common grounds with others, but it is not okay through the malicious exclusion of people who are different from us. It is fine to be people of color or white and be proud, but it is not acceptable when we pitch those who look like us against others. It is not inappropriate for people of color to associate with people of color and whites to associate with whites, but it should not be a deliberate attempt by the groups to avoid each other. Dividing groups with the swords of bias would undo man if we fail to engage common grounds constructively.

Common grounds are useful when utilized judiciously. They are natural and helpful sometimes. They are good for sorting and identifying. Geography, biology, history, social studies, and other subjects group peoples, places, cultures, and others on the basis of their relationships to each other. We may not be able to classify things easily without engaging the principle of common grounds. However, common grounds become a problem when man uses them detrimentally. Just like depraved people use race, religion, and association disapprovingly in pursuit of diabolical agenda, malicious minds have a way of manipulating every good thing for their personal agenda.

Separatist groups engage common grounds to recruit. They emphasize what unites them and some individuals, so the latter could become members of their groups. The sole aim of separatist groups is to break away from larger groups. Apart from the justifiable few who try to break away as a result of repression, many separatist leaders have their own agenda. Extremists exploit common grounds to compel people to join their groups. Known terrorist groups use religion as the basis for calling people to arm against those they perceived as enemies of faith. Gang members misuse common grounds to recruit people into their groups. They exploit race, color, regional, or neighborhood sentiments to coerce people into their gangs.

It becomes intriguing at some points when people start using common grounds desperately. Like drowning men grabbing everything around them, some create expedient common grounds for certain purposes only. I saw this happening. A group of black and white youths were in a neighborhood where I lived. Nothing pleases me more than seeing people from diverse races, religions, and cultures coming together as friends. I was thrilled to see diversity at work. However, my joy became short-lived when an elderly neighbor shared the reason behind the youths' common ground.

"It isn't what you think. Those kids are friends because they sell drugs in the neighborhood," explained the old man.

What about those who have nothing in common other than undergoing the same experiences? They could come from opposing races, religions, and social classes. It is not unusual to see former prisoners who were incarcerated in the same facilities forming common grounds after serving their terms. Just as rich people hang out together, poverty is a common ground for people. Poor people become inseparable because they belong to the same economic stratum. Before long, they start seeing those who belong to higher economic strata differently. Those who engage in the same activities sometimes enter into some form of brotherhoods.

Finding common grounds with the members of one's race, religion, or class does not constitute any problems. Crisis only starts when one provokes trouble with his identity. Identity should not lay the foundation for hatred. Whoever changes from identifying with his race, religion, or class to fighting for them irresponsibly is the problem. Those who are proud of their uniqueness are different from those who create problems with their uniqueness. He who knots himself to his group's apron without seeing anything good in others limits his horizon. Brother KKK, I am proud of being black, but the world is my constituency. Humanity is my race, and "People" is the name of my religion. I am pleased with your color, as I'm contented with mine. Notwithstanding, we remain brothers.

The more I think about them, common grounds get my attention. It is one phenomenon that man is never tired of. He continues to seek common grounds for his own survival. Sometimes, man jeopardizes initial alliances as he seeks new ones. He remains in a constant state where he hunts for alliances, looking for whatever protects his immediate interests. Man sees common grounds as the panacea when his interests are threatened. Obviously, that explains why we set aside all of our differences and came out as compatriots in the wake of the attacks on America. It was remarkable when strangers hugged and shed tears on each other's shoulders. Moments before the enemy struck, God was for all, and every man was to himself.

Common grounds look more intriguing whenever I recall what happened in New York City before the attacks. When I said "hi" to most people, they looked at me as if I had nothing better to do than look for friends. I assumed the people who did not answer my friendly gestures were not necessarily bad people. They were bowing to the norms of large cities. People are in a hurry, and they do not trust strangers because they could not differentiate bad people from good ones. However, people's fear of strangers vaporizes when sudden adversity cuts across the landmark. Strangers started hugging strangers in the street as soon as a common ground emerged. Man's instinct thinks about survival first before anything else. The attempt to survive sometimes makes man forget about the fear of strangers. Strangers become brothers impulsively.

We should adopt common grounds as a comprehensive tool for solving problems. We should not implement it to isolate others. We could sustain the consolation we found in the diverse cultures that came together on 9/11, so we can be there for each other all the time, even when God is for us all. I even want us to extend the brotherhood we found that day to the rest of mankind. Imagine the amount of succor that large doses of brotherhood would generate if smaller ones could heal cities and nations. Actually, we need each other more than we thought. All of mankind could use a huge common ground so we will not hurt one another again while searching for alliances that exclude others.

We could evolve a common ground that protects the world, not the petty common grounds that sustain the rat race culture that makes the world a planet of conflicts. I would love to see Iran respecting the existence of a Jewish state. It would be pleasing to see a sovereign Palestine that coexists side by side with a secure Israel. The fact that Jerusalem is a common ground for two tribes and three religions should prosper and not regress the region. It is fine for Arabs and Jews to coexist like the brothers they truly are. Nothing is wrong with the region attaining its tourism potentials through the religious heritages of the Wailing Wall, the Church of the Holy Sepulcher, al-Aqsa Mosque, and the Dome of the Rock.

It is not a bad idea for Iraq to live peacefully with her neighbors. It will be gratifying when a diplomatic Middle East takes its rightful position among the community of progressive regions. God might be interested in how loving, caring, and forgiving one was to fellow men, not religious bigotry.

I would love to see the United States, Syria, and Iran not play chicken anymore. North Korea would be prosperous if she would turn progressive and benefit from the blissful common ground that her neighbors enjoy. Southeast Asian nations could counter extremist groups that share common grounds with violence. Restless African nations could invest their resources in common grounds that annul poverty and conflicts. Wayward leaders would get the people's support and respect if they would turn their lives around.

The world would be a better place if man exploited common grounds for the common good of all of mankind, not egocentric purposes. It would be so pleasurable and breathtaking if powerful nations protected the interests of weak nations and did not become big brothers only when there was something in it for them.

Doing unto others exactly what we expect from them is the key to solving the world's problems. Nations that share common ground with double standards bear the burden of distrust by other nations for a long time after the deeds. Countries that sow "divide and rule" reap nothing but "divide and rule." Neither power nor might earns people respect, but impartiality, integrity, and openness do.

It would benefit Western nations if they would stop those who fleece and transfer the wealth of poor nations to the developed world. Deprived and distressed nations believe they have nothing to lose if they reach a compromise with extremists. They usually become evil's allies. A nation that has nothing except desperation shares common grounds with the wicked. The deprived nation that produces uneducated and jobless youths will become a recruiting ground for heartless radicals. A well-endowed, but rundown, nation with desperate citizens, which fleecing leaders who lack vision and mission generate, could form alliances with extremists. The world can no longer afford to have people who lose their sanity and sell their souls to the devil.

More than ever, the developed world has something to benefit from stopping the individuals and groups that pilfer from needy nations. What goes around comes around remains true. As deprived and anxious peoples migrate with their diverse baggage to flourishing nations, the developed world would share out of the consequences of the swindling of poor nations. No ocean is deep enough to stop desperate people from crossing to well-off lands. No desert is harsh enough to deter fraught peoples from reaching greener pastures. No fence is high enough to stop frantic peoples from climbing to better lives. No mountain is high enough to hold people from seeking self-esteem. No valley is low enough to stop them from searching for confidence. Who does not understand the philosophy of a desperate man?

"I'll die trying. I'll die here anyway if I don't take the risk," says the anxious mind as he departs his motherland and everything.

Developing nations at the other end of the spectrum have nothing to benefit from entering into alliances with the wicked. Forming common grounds with the malevolent is as good as turning evil. Hope would be lost and dreams would die when people sell their spirits to extremists. Life has taught me that nothing is permanent. Change is the only permanent thing I know. There is hope when you are down but not out. Keep running when the masquerader chases you. The spirit becomes tired just as the human becomes tired. You could get reprieve soon. Nature has a way of bringing down whatever goes up. Everything that is hard becomes soft at its own time. Frustrations cannot justify acts of violence. The nation that validates terrorism sells her soul, spirit, and body to the devil.

Tell those who engage the common ground of religion for murdering defenseless children and women in the name of God that the Divine is not dire. Man must quit playing the deity. There is no god except God. It is illogical for man to assume that God needs violent men to do his bidding when the Almighty is known for making things happen when he speaks. I do not know violence as a good weapon for winning any fight. Mahatma Gandhi, Martin Luther King Jr., Nelson Mandela, Gani Fawehinmi, and Aung San Suu Kyi could have lost the fights of their lives if they had engaged violence. They triumphed with nonviolence. Their names are worth plenty around the world. Any groups that engage violence should be ready to lose the fight of their lives.

Good or bad, no one starts a fight without a reason, but people lose good fights when they use bad methods. The likelihood of winning or losing a fight has to do with the method engaged. Those who sow violence in the fight of their lives would reap violence. Violence begets nothing except a vicious circle of violence. Violent groups lose friends and only gain foes. Friends turn their backs because they are not sure what the violent one would do if they became opponents in the future. The best friends today might turn into the worst enemies tomorrow. People sympathize with whoever engages nonviolence to sensitize the world, but they misunderstand the violent one. People's reactions to an initial threat sometimes determine if the world would sympathize with them or the alleged aggressors.

Violence's place is slim in the fight against injustices. The oppressed has something to show whenever the oppressor cracks the whip and the former cranks the peace. Then it is easier for the world to identify the oppressive party. However, the oppressor has something to show to the world when he exhibits the violence that the oppressed perpetrated. Nothing puts people off more than violence. People usually view violence as an overreaction on the part of a group that could have asked for the same thing diplomatically. People who want immediate reactions by substituting diplomacy with violence usually find out that the former has a way of catching up with the latter. Diplomacy could be slow, but a penny well spent is more rewarding than a pound foolishly spent.

Using nonviolence to combat acts of injustice is not weakness. It is the strongest form of civility. No scheme touches aggressors more than sensitizing their souls, spirits, and bodies with fact and tact. Every land that oppresses the meek has its own share of men and women with conscience. The conscientious have honor. The stream of fairness runs from their hearts. The time comes in the life of a nation when the conscientious rise and demand justice on behalf of the voiceless. Violence, on the other hand, sets both aggressors and the conscientious class against the violent group. Nonviolence is the passive agitator that batters the conscience, souls, spirits, and bodies of men and women without raising a finger. It pricks more than thorns and stings more than bees. It hurts more than gunshots and brings man to submission more than missiles.

Nonviolence surpasses the violent results of lethal weapons. People agitate violence with deadly weapons, but they win battles with nonviolent acts. Getting the attention of a culture with deadly weapons differs from winning the culture with acts of benevolence. People earn themselves passive enemies when they seek attention with weapons, but they win friends when they sensitize their rivals with nonviolence. Violence is not in the interest of any side of people embroiled in a war of attrition. Bloodshed portrays man as a species that is yet to make a clean break from his barbaric past. The use of weapons, in whatever quantities, to tackle issues that require diplomacy dictates that mankind remain desperate and not far from the end of his wits.

We have reached the point of no return. Nothing short of a new paradigm could save mankind. More than ever, the world needs candid voices against prejudices, fanaticism, and gang-related violence. We need voices to remind man that races, religions, and associations are not the problems. Desperate men are. Agents of polarization that put on light and search for trouble are the problem. They use everything they find to seek for trouble everywhere. Man ordains himself with the ineffectual endeavor of squeezing water out of stone. He seeks for trouble where there is none. Man finds faults in the work of nature any way he could. Man is committed to turning himself against himself without thinking about the futility of his action.

As diversity provides varieties, race does not hurt man. But man twists the beauty of nature and uses it against nature. Skin colors do not create problems, but man fashioned mischievous common grounds with those who look like him for the sole purpose of creating unnecessary divisions. He exploits the beauty of camaraderie for setting man against man. Mankind mires himself in the dire waters of intolerance and extremism unnecessarily. Man keeps searching for solutions; but he pushes deeper into the bushes of mutually assured destruction. We may be far away from sanctity, but we are close to sanity when we amend our ways and make peace with one another.

I have looked at faith, too. As much as the bad name that man gives to faith, it does not appear to present any trouble for man. Faith is an attempt to save man from hurting, but man takes religion for an unnecessary ride to the extreme. There is no compulsion in religion. But those who embrace some form of faith do so for their own good. What has man to lose when faith tries to make him responsible and stops him from engaging in substance abuse, killing the innocent, engaging in adultery, and saving himself from deadly diseases? Religion presents no problem, but the man who stretches it to the limits does. Faith does not constitute predicaments as the man who flaunts and hurts others with it.

Except when man puts it into the wrong use, association does not create a quandary either. Life becomes so unifying and rewarding when men, women, and children gather in one accord to make a difference in the world. There is resolve when people unite, not when they unite to separate from others. People get things done when they agree, not when they agree to turn against the rest of the world. Brotherhood is beautiful among the people, but it turns ugly when it becomes a tool for hurting others. Nothing is wrong with people coming together in smaller units for the common good of all, but everything is wrong with people ganging up against others.

Common ground is a double-edged sword that allows man to cut through problems, but it becomes harmful to the user if he withdraws it toward himself carelessly. Common ground is the basis for which people come together for the purpose of achieving goals. However, if they misuse it, it could also draw them back. Those who misuse common grounds for diabolical agenda, specifically to the detriment of others, lack goodwill for all, including their own groups. They are self-centered, deceptive, and injurious entities. They embrace others only when it is convenient. They dump them when there are no further reasons to hold onto them. They seek friends when it is necessary. They discard associates when they finish using them. "Divide and rule" is their tool. Manipulation is their implement. They manipulate others with racial, religious, and organizational sentiments.

Brother KKK, the time has come in mankind's history when cultures, religions, and groups have a single way forward. Man can no longer afford the luxury of polarizing the world into objectionable divisions. We need smaller entities for efficiency purposes, not racial, religious, and gang units fashioned to hurt men, women, and children. I seek no common grounds with groups that seek divisions among mankind. I pray that you, Brother KKK, would not share common grounds with groups that cherish splitting up the world. There is no room for further polarization. Instead, we need aggregates of cultures coming together for the common good of mankind.

Fair-minded people spend their time for altruistic deeds, but the prejudiced make a career out of divisive trickery. The biased are good at turning blue to red. They are fine at justifying evil deeds. Their exploits are in agreement with George

Aiken's observation that bigots would find a way to justify prejudice if they would find out one morning that the whole world was made of one race. They give no thought to the beauty of diversity and camaraderie among men. Their sole goal is to hide behind racial curtains and stop man from reconciling with mankind. Bigots have mastered the art of exploiting common grounds to set people against people. They reserve brotherhood for their kinds, and they wish the rest of mankind destruction and death.

Brother KKK, failure is not an option as the world journeys into the twelfth hour. Mankind is staggering at the rim of an apocalyptic abyss. The day of reckoning is beckoning. Clouds are gathering over our shared destiny. Our children's future is yearning for help. Tolerance is the only common ground that is capable of escorting man back to sanity. Let the common ground of peace traverse all the continents known to man. Let unity sail across the seven seas. The tranquil draft of harmony should blow around the hills of the continents. Man must know peace in the Caribbean, Europe, Greenland, Middle East, and Pacific Ocean. Common grounds shall no longer be tools for isolating peoples. They will be an efficient apparatus for unity in diversity. Our children should not form common grounds with gangsters that generate nothing except consternation for fellow men.

CHAPTER 8

▼

GANG FACTOR

Give to us clear vision that we may know where to stand and what to stand for because unless we stand for something, we shall fall for anything.
—Peter Marshall

Brother KKK, I am compelled to tell you the story that takes the breath out of me every time it comes to memory. Little Joe was an adorable creature, a picture-perfect image of Cupid on earth. His bewitching smile complemented his attractive face. The women in his neighborhood built castles in the air while fantasizing they were his mothers. Prospective fathers in the precinct allowed their imaginations to run wild as they imagined they were his fathers. Joe lacked a remarkable wardrobe, but every material looked good on him. Everyone thought he was smart because he was streetwise. Joe was not an average student at school either. He had all it took to become a leader. In fact, many saw him as a future town council member or member of the House of Representatives. He could be a senator if he wanted. Some even thought he was a prospective governor or a potential president. A blissful future kept beckoning and smiling at Joe. He seemed to have found his niche.

Joe's parents were not rich, but he was lucky to be born in America. The sky was the limit for every child who cared about moving forward in this country. If he worked for it, he could secure scholarships for college. Savvy youngsters could get low-interest government and institutional loans. If he could not go to college, Joe could even learn some productive vocation. His parents were not the best role models ever, but his city was not short of positive ones. Enough nonprofit organizations helped kids like Joe around the city. He sometimes did not have all that he wanted to eat, but he was not hungry either. Compared to many children around the world, it appeared like fate cracked his nuts for him.

It was so troublesome that the growing boy lacked clear vision about where to stand in life. He did not know what to stand for. Joe was about to fall for anything. He could have hung out with good students at the local school, but he chose to associate with the gangsters on campus. He was not in a gang initially, but he soon joined the ranks of wannabes. He later connected to the fledgling bullies at his school. The once-charming kid started falling short of the sweet manners that set him apart from many students on campus and in his neighborhood. One of Joe's teachers was the first to notice the struggling child as he teetered between the roads to success and failure.

"The road to failure is not for you, Joe," the passionate and unrelenting teacher told him for the umpteenth time.

"This is my life. Leave me alone," said Joe under his breath.

The unsuspecting boy misconstrued the freedom enjoyed by millions of his countrymen, women, and children to mean that he could live his life the way he chose. He had no idea that life was too precious for anyone to waste. Joe could not figure out that the difference between making it in life and losing it all were the seemingly harmless, but decidedly detrimental, choices that people make. He thought he knew it all, but he did not realize that life was a lifetime school for learning until one died. Joe started disliking the persistent teacher who refused to give up on him. He could not understand why the meddling teacher could not just mind her own business. He failed to heed the free-flowing advice that came his way. His parents even accused the good teacher of picking on him.

The fast-degenerating boy joined the gang that he had been claiming. He barely realized the danger he was dragging himself into until he reached the blind spot that many gangsters usually end up at after thinking they were in control. Joe had barely spent a semester in the high school when fellow gangsters asked him to cruise with them along the city's main boulevard during a local festivity. He could not ask for more as he gladly hopped into his homey's car. The quivering music in the car mixed with the turbo-charged noise from the silencer made life a deafening hell for other road users. Joe, wearing his baseball cap backward, as if that confirmed why he was taking life backward, had heard about drive-by shootings, but he had yet to witness one. A fellow passenger pulled the trigger and killed a rival gang member as they cruised through a dodgy neighborhood after bouts of marijuana use.

Like a bad dream, the jury pronounced Joe guilty of murder a few months later. Police officers had found the evidence inside his pocket. Minutes before police caught up with them, the shooter had given the pistol to Joe to hold. The killer deceitfully told the court that Joe pulled the trigger. The remaining gangsters in the car substantiated the shooter's statement because they were afraid of him.

"The road to failure is not for you, Joe," his teacher once said.

The trembling teenager heard his former teacher's voice booming in his head as a police officer slipped a pair of handcuffs around his wrists after his sentencing. Joe suddenly saw his life faltering violently before his very own eyes. Life stood still as Joe wished he could turn back time and make things up to himself. It was too late. People seldom had their cakes after eating them. The bad dream did not look real to claustrophobic Joe until the heavy steel doors clanged behind him in a lonely, concrete cell.

The distraught young man remained in a state of denial for most of the night.

"It can't be," he tried to reassure himself as the conscious part of his brain convinced him that he would be behind the cold bars for a very long time.

Joe tried to blame his parents for not being good role models. However, he recalled that his teacher repeatedly told the class that it would be about them, not their parents, in years to come. The teacher had told them the story of the young boys who trekked hundreds of miles without their parents to get away from the ravaging war in their country. The teacher said the boys' parents died in the war, but many of them survived on their own. They were even successful years later.

"The orphans that trekked hundreds of miles without shoes made it, but I failed to make it from home to school with my shoes on," cried Joe.

His brain pushed aside thoughts about him for a moment. Instead, he focused on the orphans' traumatized journey to survival. He imagined the kids using the little equipment they had to get what they wanted instead of whining about not having so much. Joe was sure the kids did not have any real food as they journeyed. They could not afford any luxuries. It was a matter of lonely souls crying for survival without shedding tears. On that day, Joe unintentionally took stock as he hung his head in his hands and cried. He looked messed up with his face smeared with tears and mucus from his nostrils.

Joe regretted that several adults had tried to play his parents' roles and he had not paid attention to them. He was sorry for becoming belligerent when his school's administrators tried to intervene in his life. Joe was filled with disgust for himself when he recalled how rude he was to the teacher that tried to help him. He could not stand himself for instigating other students to be discourteous to the teacher that could have been his savior. He had alleged that the teacher had singled him out. Joe realized he could have become a different person if he had tried. Nothing made him angry with himself more than the realization that fellow gang members took advantage of him. They only called him a friend when it was convenient for them, but they lied to save themselves when the law caught up with them. Joe succeeded in falling for anything, and he had to pay for it.

He concluded that his life was a wasted one. He would be about sixty years old before qualifying for parole, but he was not sure that he would ever get one. Joe could not stop grieving over his bungled life. The formerly popular kid on campus shared his life with people whose lives were equally messed up. The good-looking boy was now a ghost of his old self. After a few weeks in prison, Joe's wrinkled face, combined with his sunken eyes, made him look twice as old as his real age. He could not forgive himself for squandering his shrewdness on negativity when he could have invested it in progress.

"I thought I knew everything. I refused to accept directions from adults. Now, I'm lost," he lamented.

Brother KKK, I am relieved to inform you that Joe did not exist, but I am nervous to remind you that there are many little Joes in our cities. They are wannabes who lack clear vision about where to stand and what to stand for in life. They might fall for anything in the end. Desperate gangsters that take advantage of naïve followers lure innocent youths to the vicious world of crime and violence. Ranking members of gangs come with the pretense of providing families for youngsters who lack loving and caring homes. But they have nothing to offer the unsuspecting youths besides criminality. Highly placed members of gangs use younger members to achieve their criminal goals. High-ranking members of gangs sometimes have the impression that they are protecting their neighborhoods without looking at the larger picture of the danger they constitute.

Gangsters take advantage of followers that lack the ability to distinguish between what they did and did not want. Followers rarely realize they have the liberty and freedom to make their own choices without interference from friends. They agree with everything their friends suggest without realizing that the latter make wrong judgments, too. The low-esteemed wannabes might say that they join because of lack of love at home. But these reasons cannot stand. They could affiliate with lawful and supportive groups instead of gangs. Many new members join gangs because they want friends, but they do not realize they could choose good friends instead of gangsters. Some expect to have fun by joining gangs without grasping the fact that people have more fun when they engage in lawful activities.

Followers without vision do not recognize the fact that they could be recognized, too, by creating positive trends without following those who turn their backs on society. Why seek acceptance from the needlessly disgruntled members of society when they could create positive trends on their own? Why should people seek protection from people who destroy people? Why do wannabes allow peer pressure to push them around when they could remain confident boys and girls on their own? Should people seek reputation through the humiliating blind alley of lawlessness when a reputable boulevard of fame is ahead of them? Why do clever people waste their intelligence through committing vices with losers when they could generate goodwill with winners? Wannabes have neither thrill nor satisfaction from taking the wrong route, but they just get an unpleasant encounter with the law in the end.

Wannabes are the "use and dump" cadres who do the dirty jobs of the ranking members of gangs. Many hardly make it to the levels where they become famous or make illegal money like the top members. They usually find themselves in prison, maimed for life, or even killed without getting to the top. Joining gangs is not a good prescription for poverty-stricken youths. There is no alternative way to making hassle-free money than earning it lawfully. Any shortcut to wealth is a potential short route to long-term imprisonment. Joining gangs to survive could be a good way of denying oneself continued existence. Gangs and good things of life hardly stay together for long. Gang paraphernalia scare away good friends. Law-abiding people do not go near gang-related bandannas and jewelry.

Gangsters are bound to lose more than they invest in illegal association. Because of their poor attitudes to education, they rarely have academic or vocational certifications that employers require. Gang-related tattoos, ornaments, clothing, and attitudes betray their owners. Employers are not fond of offering jobs to those who have them. Business owners understand that gang members are associated with illegal activities. Lawful business managers do not offer jobs to those who carry deadly and illegal weapons. Bosses do not cherish dealing with violence-oriented subordinates either. Most businesses keep jobs away from people who use gang signs and slang. Gangs and illegal drug users are associates, but they do not mix with positive work ethics. People do not come to work regularly after a night out of alcohol and illegal drug consumption.

Brother KKK, can you see the dilemma the world is facing? The evils that gangs generate are leading to sleepless nights in our cities. Rival gangs and drug dealers are forcing families to grieve over lost loved ones. Children are turning to dangerous drugs. Many youths are stealing to sustain destructive drug habits. Government is needlessly spending substantial amounts of money to fix vandalism and graffiti that gangsters create. To avoid threats from gangs, businesses are fleeing from communities. Drive-by shooters are endangering people. Physical attacks of defenseless youths are on the rise. Gang bullies are making life miserable for students in school hallways. Formerly peaceful communities are becoming restless. Governments are running from pillars to posts to save youths from themselves.

Why does a gang entice clever people? A gang is a family that thrives on illegality and violence. It is the family that welcomes aspirants but disowns its own when pushing becomes shoving. Real people understand that the sibling rivalries within a gang and the hassles between gangs are not worth the risk. Gang members undercut one another for reputation and positions in the absence of rival gangs to fight with. Gangs jostle for prominence and territories at all times. Cruel beatings at gang initiations relegate humans to beasts without any feelings. Instead of getting protection, youths seeking protection become endangered species of human beings. Formerly responsible youths turn their backs on society. People who seek cheap money find cheap death. But why does a gang attract youths?

Stanley "Tookie" Williams III reportedly cofounded the *Crips*, the street gang that began from Los Angeles in the early 1970s. His supposed intent was to sanitize his neighborhood in an unconventional way, but the events that followed years later swallowed him. Williams tried to be good through the only way he knew. He apparently meant well in the beginning, but taking an aggressive route to create charity for the people was a mistake. Violence has no business with putting smiles on people's faces. One of the worst mistakes a man could make is to create ogres for his own protection. Whoever creates monsters could end up in his creation's bowels someday.

There comes a time in the life of a man when pragmatism catches up with radicalism and maturity topples immaturity. Williams was not an exception. He acknowledged personal redemption. He even became an anti-gang activist while in prison. He wrote outstanding books, discouraging youths from joining gangs. It took hard work to write books.

"To err is for human and to forgive is Divine," they say.

Williams regretted founding a gang, but he did not receive any forgiveness as he offended man and not the Divine. Who says it is not better to offend the Divine than to affront fellow humans? The murders he reportedly committed during his heyday did not give him a chance. What is in a gang if the cofounder of a hard-hitting gang could renounce it?

The State of California did not accept Williams' emancipation from his past, even though many believed his redemption was real. Before dawn on December 13, 2005, he paid the supreme price with his life by lethal injection at San Quentin State Prison, California. Williams sent words to those with clear vision to show wannabes where to stand and what to stand for. Else, they would fall for anything.

He wrote, "The war within me is over. I battled my demons, and I was triumphant. Teach them how to avoid our destructive footsteps. Teach them to strive for higher education. Teach them to promote peace. And teach them to focus on rebuilding the neighborhoods that you, others, and I helped to destroy."

Brother KKK, you and I have a mission. A colossal undertaking lies ahead of us. Let's tutor the young ones on how to wrestle the demons in them and come out victorious. We must edify them on keeping away from the disparaging blunders that our generation committed. The new generations of mankind should not tread the caustic route that the older generation created. It is time to rebuild the world that the generations before us disillusioned by and we further devastated. Let's cut olive branches for our youths. The world needs peacemakers, not those who generate violence. What if we embrace realism and forsake extremism. What if we teach peace to our children? The time has come for maturity to topple immaturity. Gangs must embrace peace now in one accord.

Gangs are products of the societies to which they belong. Whoever mothered a defiant child should have to carry him on his back. Societies that mothered restless youths should calm their frays. Let all grown-ups go on self-imposed mission of freeing our youths from the shackles of gangs. On this issue, fathers must talk to their children, and mothers should remain on the same page with their men. Gangs only create grief, not wealth or fun, in the long run. We cannot sow trouble and anguish and plan to reap joy and contentment. Think of legacies to bequeath children. Gangs should not come to mind. Violence and illegal drug deals should not be parting gifts to our youths. The priceless jewels of society should not inherit aggression and insecurity.

Our generation was once young and immature, Brother KKK. Now we have come of age and matured. We were once restless and irresolute. Now we are focused and decisive. Brutality and illegality should no longer be parts of our baggage. Maturity and diplomacy should be our watchwords. Our youths are crying for care, courtesy, skills, sobriety, restraint, and reverence. Let's give what the youths need and offer them what they deserve. The world is yearning for love, light, peace, prosperity, unity, and understanding. Let there be love in homes, peace in the streets, and unity in neighborhoods. There should be light for the youths to see. Prosperity must be their goal. Understanding should be their watchword.

Many justified gangs as some of the fallout from an agitated world. They tied the prevalence of street gangs to the mismanagement of younger generations by older generations. Others wanted every generation to stand accountable for its shortcomings. Whatever side of the aisle you belonged, Brother KKK, we have one goal ahead of us. Does it matter if a man spots a venomous snake and a woman puts it away? All that matters is for someone to stop the poisonous creature from hurting defenseless children. The leaders of tomorrow deserve better things than sadism and anguish. Gangs should not relegate our youths to the wilderness of revulsion. Never again shall gangs empty the dreams of thirsty youths in their prime. Our children's aspirations should not vanish like mirages that offer no sips to thirsty lips.

Brother KKK, here's my take on the gang debate. Whatever cannot produce happiness cannot make one happy indefinitely. Violence would not make youths feel better if it cannot create contentment. Illegal drug use cannot spawn real fun if perdition is the only destination it offers one-way tickets to. Short-lived pleasure without peace of mind should not attract our youths. Gang membership cannot be the therapy for youths who lack family support. The world is a family of dutiful, cheerful, and hopeful youths. Lack of parents is not an excuse for orphans to adopt the devil as a father. Those who adopt gangs as their families should prepare for lifetimes of broken dreams. Serpents do not give birth to doves. Gangs bequeath nothing except violence and broken lives.

Tragically, youths sell their dreams and aspirations to gangs, who stop the journey a few feet away from the bend that separates them and victory. Nobody lacks the ability to do something right, but many lack the ability to dare. Many drop equitable ambitions on the rigid concrete of disbelief in themselves and shatter all that providence offered them with no strings attached. Possibility is the middle name of those who believe in themselves. I challenge every youth who craves success to dare to step to the next stage when the journey seems torturous and the stakes appear high. Those who refuse to trade their lives for gangs will someday soar like eagles in the limitless skies of accomplishment. He who cuts corners to wealth could be cutting corners to humiliation.

There is more to life than instant gratification that violence and criminality institute. I would rather be an honorable servant in a petite castle of honor than a king in a mammoth castle of dishonor. I would rather bear loneliness with grace than share my body, soul, and spirit with a hoard of friends who thrive on transgression and mayhem. Anarchy will not benefit from my goodwill. Criminality will not enjoy my friendship. Let the rat at home hear and tell the one in the bush. The bird in the house should hear and inform the one outside that gangs have no share in my children's lives. My neighborhood is not large enough for gangsters and me. The bandit that hops into the backyard of a no-nonsense man has one more hopping to do as the latter kicks him out. Not in my backyard, gangsters.

I do not have either fortune or chattels, but I offer everything I have to distressed youths everywhere. Please accept my respect and heart of gold. Cope and hold on to hope as dope ropes people into holes. The world is not against you. Fair-minded people everywhere share your pains. Remember, you are the hope of tomorrow and the trustees of a peaceful future. By no means should you lose sight of the honor bestowed on those who behold hope. Be the silent workers who cement a fractured world. You are the sweeteners. Without you, the world would remain bitter. Become the good leaders of tomorrow as the world is weary of leadership blues. Let me depart with a word to those who give up hope for dope. I seek not to condemn stressed youths, the hope of tomorrow, and trustees of a beautiful future. I seek to condemn the brutal and the criminal.

Viocracy
Ripping through our sphere like a warring tornado
Mustering strength to daunt a weary world
Draping lands and climes like iron curtains
Separating youths from civility and propriety
Violence of the youth by the youth and for the youth
Viocracy!

A moment of moral crisis for irate youths
Who set violence loose and blame frustration
Fly emotional kites into a rage and wreck peace
Surrender reasoning to eloquence of violence
Address wrong with wrong and get wrong
Viocracy!

An eye for an eye would leave us all blind
Alter anger to courage, the constructive weapon
Bear frustration without betraying emotion
You are the hope of a peaceful tomorrow
Say no to violence of the youth for the youth
Viocracy!

CHAPTER 9

▼

LEADERSHIP BLUES

It is not only what we do, but also what we do not do, for which we are accountable.
—Jean-Baptiste Poquelin

Brother KKK, I pray you are enjoying my long missive. I am pregnant with words and laboring to deliver. I know that words hurt the stomach, like pregnancy, if not delivered. My belly is filled with speeches as the quiver of a seasoned hunter is filled with arrows. My poultry swarms with words. Some of the words are warming up to incubate tolerance. Some are hatching, and the hatchery is coming up with restraint. I can tell that some are already raring broad-minded-ness. I cannot stop thinking about passing some words to those who decide the fate of this weary world. Someone should alert the community of conscientious leaders about the laborious, but gratifying, work ahead. Administrators of places of worship must fortify themselves for the arduous, but rewarding, labor to come. Churches, mosques, synagogues, and shrines must give a wide berth to hatred, violence, and divisions among mankind. Atheists have work to do, too. Let's remake the world. Mother Earth is crying for social justice, tolerance, and harmony. Integrity has to become man's first-rate friend.

What about a story to illustrate why those who do not want to become miracle workers should not lead? Once upon a time, all warriors began a journey to the land of spirits to give stewardship of their roles in a weary world. They came in splendor and opulence, carried within exquisite palanquins of many colors. Trumpets blared. Overzealous servants whipped ordinary people away from the route.

"Make way for special people!" they yelled at the top of their voices.

The sun shined with all of its brilliance. Clouds did not have any chance of stealing the day from the mighty and powerful. It appeared like nature consented to honoring the warriors on their way to the palace of the king of spirits. Rain and winds were away from the streets. Only the dust that the multitude of feet generated connected the earth to heaven.

Surrounded by his chiefs, the king of all spirits awaited the earthly warriors. Compared to earthly palaces, the palace of the king of spirits was more beautiful in all standards. Compared to those in the land of spirits, earthly gold, diamond, and sapphire did not have a chance. The king's trumpet blowers were the best ever. His henchmen were even powerful and stronger than earthly warriors, but they did not whip ordinary people. Decked in gold and priceless jewels of immeasurable prices, the king's throne sparkled like dazzling stars. The sun, moon, and stars bowed down before him. All awed him in trepidation! The earthly warriors' yes-men became fearful as they approached the gate of the city of spirits. The coming of earthly warriors before the king of spirits appeared like the visit of toothless rats before a gigantic lion.

The warriors and the yes-men searched their souls and sang as they approached the gate of spirits, "What did I do wrong? Let me make right now before entering his presence. Offenders cannot stand by him. The king of spirits is just. What did I do wrong?"

The warriors and their yes-men suddenly became powerless as the gatekeeper waved his magic wands.

"Silence! Silence! Silence!" yelled the gatekeeper

Worldly judges were about to enter the city of the judge of the spirits. The concierge opened the gates for the warriors, but he denied access to their entourages.

"Everyone must stand before the king by himself," insisted the doorkeeper.

The warriors' entourages did not have any options besides returning to where they belonged, leaving the once-powerful men to their fates. The earthly warriors were about to experience what the least among their citizens experienced on earth. Change became the only thing permanent for the warriors.

Maybe the most tortuous among man's misfortunes is his potential to forget so soon. He learns little from history and falls for the same things that he witnessed those before him fell for. The yes-men forgot about their masters' misfortune at the gate of the land of spirits. They installed mean fellows as new warriors as soon as they returned to their diverse kingdoms. Everyone returned to business as usual once again. Only bootlickers got the new warriors' ears. Overzealous henchmen did not stop harassing ordinary people when the new warriors hit the streets. The henchmen worked tirelessly to outsmart one another as they struggled to please their masters. The business of intrigue appeared like the only language that was understood along the corridors of power.

One by one, the old warriors came before the king of the land of spirits in order to give stewardship of their roles in a weary world. The warrior of the land where a few citizens turned radicals and terrorized the world was the first to come before the judge of the land of spirits. He was confident that the king of spirits would not find anything wrong with how he administered his people. But he shuddered like a frightened child caught in a monsoon windstorm. He felt lonely and miserable. His old powers were gone. He swallowed saliva repeatedly to moisten his dry throat while struggling to stand still.

The warrior murmured the song as he approached the throne, "What did I do wrong? Let me make right now before entering his presence. Offenders cannot stand by him. The king of spirits is just. What did I do wrong?"

The king of the land of spirits heard the song and roared like a warring lion. All things around him trembled and bowed in apprehension. Silence traversed the land of spirits without much ado.

"Why did you become a radical and terrorize my creations?" asked the judge of the land of spirits.

"Glory to the king!" shouted the king's men in unison. "The king's reign shall never end!"

Undoubtedly, the king of spirits had absolute power over all things that existed. Good and bad spirits alike feared him. He had power over life and death. He could make anything he desired to come to pass. His words were like sharpened swords. They cut through whatever they struck.

The worldly, but terrified and surprised, warrior could not believe his ears and began, "Your Honor, I was only the warrior. I did not terrorize the world. A few of my citizens committed the crime for which I'm charged."

The warrior did not understand why he should pay for the crimes that some of his followers committed. He tried to no avail to distinguish himself from the vile exploits of his followers, forgetting that he who does not want to make decisions should not be a leader. Someone must take responsibility for the collective actions of a group. That person is not usually an ordinary follower. He is the one who took the praise when things went well. The warrior was yet to understand how everything worked after all.

"Whoever said you were not liable for the crimes committed by your followers was wrong," interrupted the king of the land of spirits. "You had the authority, but you did little to stop your followers from terrorizing my creatures."

He neither listened to the outlandish excuses nor the explanations that people advanced. He knew more than any human aspired to know. His understanding surpassed those of the best among men. The king of spirits could see through man. His knowledge of what was inside men made X-rays look inferior. Nothing was strange to him. Everything that man could not see remained clear to him. All that existed happened at his pleasure. The king of spirits was everything, and everything was he.

The once-powerful warrior stood before the king and tried to justify his role in a weary world. He pleaded, "I tried to be upright and did not terrorize your creatures, your honor."

The warrior wished he were having a very bad dream. He even wondered if he could turn back time to amend the omission.

"A warrior is not answerable only to what he did. He pays for what he left undone, too," insisted the king of the land of spirits. "You have no idea how many naïve youths blew up themselves and innocent people for nothing, believing that they would go to heaven."

He ordered the warrior to serve an endless term of chastisement because he did not do enough to stop his followers from fomenting violence.

The warrior who had the clout, but lacked the will, to instill social justice in the world came next before the king of the land of spirits. He sang the same song and argued the same way as the first warrior.

"Do you remember the endless rhetoric you made about making the world a happy place for all and sundry?" the king reminded him He took him back to the empty talks he held with fellow warriors about banishing injustice from the surface of the earth.

"What about when you harbored stolen wealth from pitiable lands, as a result, innocent children died of hunger. You supplied deadly weapons to lands that needed food. Do you remember the toxic waste you exported to helpless nations," recalled the king of spirits.

The latter received the same judgment as the first warrior.

Then came the warrior who stole from his own people and hid the booty in other lands. "Provide an explanation for your wicked and disgraceful action," requested the king. The warrior realized he did not need all of the stolen wealth after all. Rich and poor people were the same in the land of spirits. Besides, the warrior came to the land of spirits before he could put the stolen riches into any use.

"Didn't you hear that vanity upon vanity is vanity?" asked the king.

The king reminded the warrior about the hardship he exposed his country's opposition leaders to. There was no hiding place for the warrior's golden fish. He looked foolish and powerless before the lion that could devour without consequences.

"I'll right every wrong if you give me just one more chance, Your Honor," begged the warrior.

"There are no more chances once people cross over to the land of spirits. You cannot escape from the consequences designed for your immoral actions. See the traumatized faces of innocent children who died of starvation because you stole the money meant for their upkeep. Can't you see the faces of multitudes of youths who lost everything because you squandered their future?" rebuked the king of spirits.

The king revealed the infrastructure in disrepair in the formerly well-heeled nation that the warrior administered. He ordered him to an infinite term of reprimand.

There was a modest and selfless warrior with a human face. He thought about his people first and placed their priorities above his own. He guarded his people's wealth like his own baby. He spent their money plausibly like his own. He knew the meaning of patriotism and knew that leadership was a serious business. He understood that leadership was worth taking criticism for. It was even worth dying for. The warrior did not expect people who were not miracle workers to lead. He did not start out as a miracle worker, but his tireless efforts to be fair and just in his commissions and omissions made him a miracle worker. He was a commonplace fellow. He did not have the blood of royalty running in his veins, but he was a real hero to the people he devoted a lifetime of service to.

The good warrior was human, too. He fidgeted as the king of spirits ordered him to step before the throne to chronicle his roles in a weary world. He knew he tried his best while leading his people, but he was not sure if his best was good enough. He hesitated involuntarily as he treaded the ruby grounds of the palace of the king of spirits. The warrior recalled how some of his chiefs tried to blackmail him when he stopped them from duping the people. He remembered how he stood his grounds when corrupt chiefs tried to force the state to fund shady projects. He recollected that he did not project his family and friends above the ordinary people of his land. The good warrior knew he gave injustice a wide berth in all of its ramifications.

He hummed the usual song as he approached the unmovable king of spirits, "What did I do wrong? Let me make right now before entering his presence. Offenders cannot stand by him. The king of spirits is just. What did I do wrong?"

"Welcome to the infinite pleasure reserved for leaders with mission and vision," declared the king of spirits delightfully. "It takes insightful people to surrender worldly vanities for the ceaseless gratifications that follow."

The formidable king offered a generous handshake to the deserving warrior. The king waved his magic wand so the warrior could see the contented faces of the people of his kingdom back on earth. The people were mournful, but they decided to celebrate the life and times of their departed warrior. Young and old alike spoke generously about the thoughtful warrior that placed his people's concerns above his own. People in the streets eagerly praised the benevolent warrior. There was joy in the land of spirits, too. All spirits struggled to shake hands with the wise warrior who refused to fall for what those before him fell for.

All except the judicious warrior lived regretfully thereafter. They could not make appeals once the king of spirits delivered his judgment. The vanities that the powerful and mighty amassed were nothing except self-deceit.

Imagine your community's warrior and my neighborhood's warrior coming before the king of the land of spirits some day. There would be a lot of explanations for the ups and downs in our weary world. Many warriors would have to explain what turned the beautiful world to a weary world. Some would argue that it takes a miracle worker to tread the road of life without tilting his head somehow. Nevertheless, there is no compulsion in public positions. Whoever does not want to be a miracle worker should not lead. The voice of the people is the voice of the Divine. Whatever leaders promised the people, they pledged to the Divine, too. Let elected officials reflect before promising the people. They promise the Divine whatever they promise the people. No one gets away with what he owes the Divine.

What about a friendly reminder to those who decide the fate of our weary world? What would they tell the king of the land of spirits if they would find themselves in the warriors' tight shoes? What would the billionaire leader who had no moneymaking business prior to governing the people tell the king of spirits? Could he justify the millions of dreams that his commission or omission killed? Would he look at the numerous faces of blameless children who died as a result of an egocentric leader? What about the uncountable families he destroyed when jobless youths became armed robbers and murdered breadwinners? How is the leader going to explain the derision he brought on his people and nation after he stole so much and left his country underdeveloped? It will be tough for pilfering leaders.

Imagine what awaits the leader who talks about justice for all but harbors wealth stolen from destitute nations? As long as money comes out of the deals, this leader sees the world in term of business only and does not mind selling weapons for destroying inopportune children and defenseless oppositions in pitiable nations. Would he look at the faces of the infant victims of his action? What about his indifference to injustice in nations that he trades with? Imagine the number of orphans generated by his exploits when jobless parents died of heartaches. What would the leader tell his own children if they would ask him why his action led to the death of many children? What if they would ask their father why the blatant acts of injustice occurred under his nose? Picture the amount of goodwill he squandered when deprived nations started blaming their woes on his nation and people. What would the king of the land of spirits tell the leader? It would be ugly.

Would the leader who granted free reign to terrorists stand before the king of the land of spirits? Would he justify the excruciating death of innocent children as fair game? Would the leader that encouraged killings on the basis of religion be able to convince the king of the land of spirits? Could the preacher who preached hatred when the books talked about love win the heart of the king of spirits? What if love is the only religion that the king recognizes? Imagine if compassion is the only creed that appeases him? What if forgiveness is the single doctrine that thrills him? What would the leader who hated on the basis of race tell the king of the land of spirits? What if the king is neither black nor white? It would be grim for some. But it would be poignant for others. Many leaders would envy the judgments handed to the least among their citizens. Some would wish they were never born.

Leadership is worth taking seriously. It is heavy and worth its weight in gold. It is not a vehicle for securing popularity or enriching oneself. Leadership should never be a means for doubling one's wealth. There is more to leading than abusing the power that comes with it. Leaders should not lead because of marble houses. They are only servants of the people. Service should be to leadership what Mother Teresa was to India. Caring should be to world managers what Mahatma Gandhi meant to nonviolence. Fairness should be to rulers what Martin Luther King Jr. was to peacefulness. Abuse of authority and all of its accompaniments should be strange to monarchs. Misuse of influence and all of its trappings would make sovereigns tremble before the king of spirits.

Wine would not flow for inequitable warriors when they go before the king of the spirits, but tears, sweat, and blood would stream. Pomp and pageantry would be absent, but there would be enough of regrets and distress to go around. Yes-men would turn the circle and testify against their masters. Fair-weather friends and business associates shall deny the warriors and all that they stood for.

There would be no marble houses for those who made the world a weary place. Unjust warriors shall be powerless before the defenseless children who died as a result of their insensitive actions. The warriors' children would disown them. Their spouses would declare them as *persona non grata*. The world shall not weep for them. The sun shall not shine for them. Stars shall not twinkle for them. Warriors should be ready to give accounts of their roles in a weary world.

I have an idea, Brother KKK. We could become emissaries of hope for mankind. You and I could be partners in reminding leaders about the reasons why they were leaders. What if we tell egocentric rulers to stop being childish and start acting like grown people? What if we notify radical preachers to renounce radicalism and cuddle pragmatism? We could teach insufferable leaders how to love and disallow them from tutoring their children how to hate. You and I could show leaders the sense behind investing in integration than sowing in disintegration. What does it profit the man who lives for a speck of years in an endless continuum of eternity to hate and leave nothing behind except the shame attached to his name?

Irrational leaders should comprehend that hatred would never be virtuous if it has never been and would never be. What is the benefit of the cola that lacks nutritious value and tastes bitter? Hatred has no moral value and always remains bitter. Let inequitable leaders put their conscience to the test and quit holding onto the straw of hatred. Thoughtful leaders understand that the first sometimes becomes the last and the last becomes the first. The governor would one day become the governed. Change makes the world an interesting place. Nothing remains forever for mortal man. The unjust leaders of our time would get their dates before the king of spirits.

It is right for leaders to make right what they did wrong. Going before the king of spirits in golden caskets does not guarantee free passages. Lying in marble tombs does not lead to the king's revered guesthouse. Offenders will not stand by him. Unfair leaders cannot withstand his wrath. Rich and famous cannot buy favor from him. The king of spirits is just. Monarchs and sovereigns cannot pay their ways to his kingdom. He will not tolerate chiefs with penchants for intolerance. Corrupt yes-men would not enter through the gates of his palace. It is time for reality checks. Let all warriors check where they stand. It should be clear that there is no appealing once man crosses the fast-flowing Rubicon across the road to the land of spirits.

Brother KKK, you will agree that some of the men and women who run our weary world are not miracle workers. The world needs miracle workers, not impeccable talkers who speak articulately without results. A man may not be born a miracle worker, but his bids and deeds may turn out to be events from the realm of miracles. Man is not great by his looks or size. It is his propositions and actions that matter. Talks do not make leaders great, but genuine thoughts make them stand out. Contemporary leaders should pay less attention to power and authority, but they should take their bids and deeds more seriously. Wealth and assets should not be the underlying goals for leading, but authentic calls to service should determine who leads. Neither silver nor gold makes a great leader, but a mind of silver and a heart of gold make a renowned leader.

The old and weary world needs leaders who speak from their hearts and mean every word that proceeds from their mouths. Eloquence of words without positive bids and deeds would not advance human cause. Leaders must have done something terribly wrong if terrorism has become a universal phenomenon that limits man's freedom everywhere. Past and present leaders got it wrong somewhere if nations are so deprived and becoming breeding grounds for terrorists. Leadership has degenerated if leaders are robbing their own countries entirely. Social justice has no place in our world if nations are abetting and harnessing the wealth stolen from nations where children are dying of curable diseases. Unless Mother Nature changes her way, the world cannot ask for all the tranquility that she could offer.

Mankind began the twenty-first century with elevated cultural, religious, and gang tensions. Leaders spent more time on things that did not matter. Suspicion among people with diverse ways of life rose to an all-time high when leaders engaged cultures and religions for personal agenda. Man has continued to mistrust man over the past decade because leaders set the tone of mistrust. Violence became a borderless phenomenon that haunts every human through the commission and omission of leaders. Threats by gangs are not departing from our cities. Nonviolent neighborhoods are becoming agitated. How long would the peace-loving majority of the people around the world submit to these undesirable trends?

Blessed are the living warriors who are willing to make up for their wrongs. They are not going before the king of spirits yet. There is time to patch up the wrongs and soothe the multitude of toes they stepped on unjustifiably. To err is human. Whoever makes up for his wrongs has a chance of receiving reprieve. A thousand-mile journey to absolution begins with a genuine stride of contrition. It may not be late for the living who reaches the turning point, rights the wrongs he committed, and seeks clemency from the right quarters. It is rational to expect the magnanimous king of spirits to absolve warriors who right the wrongs they commit before coming to the land of spirits. Erring warriors could take responsibility for their blunders and right the wrongs they committed before departing the weary world.

Everything that exists has its time and term. There is a time to enter and a time to exit the world. There is a time to begin and a time to end. There is a time to sow and a time to reap. Hatred has its time. Love has its time. There is a time to offend and a time to forgive. There is a time for hurting and a time for healing. There comes a time when the conscientious among men arrive at a turning point and redress the wrongs they originated. It is time for the managers of the weary world to become miracle workers. Let leaders set the tone for the healing to begin. It is right for people to acknowledge and remedy past wrongdoings so old wounds and pains could heal. Let forgiveness of the people, by the people, and for the people commence. Mankind would hopelessly and endlessly cling to the agonizing history of mistrust if some fail to redress old wrongs and others fail to reach the turning point of forgiveness.

Leaders can only respond as the tired and worn ships of the world continue to take water from the torturous sea of uncertainty. Governments distrust governments; nations distrust nations. Races are mad at races; religions irritate one another. The world walks on its head as preachers advocate hatred and the faithful continue to kill in the name of an all-loving God. Leaders address social injustices with eloquence of words without corresponding fluency of actions. Rulers are disconnected from their peoples as yes-men tell them that all is well when so much is wrong. Years of dithering should give way to years of listening. Leaders should listen twice before they speak once to their peoples.

Look around you, Brother KKK. Time is fading for negligent leadership. World leaders are dishing out politics instead of policies that unite nations. People do not appreciate what they have until they no longer have them. Current leaders would lose their powers and cease to be leaders some day. Let them right old wrongs before they lose the influence to do so. The years of leadership blues must end. We need real leadership. The epoch of politics without inspiring policies should not tarry. The era of leaders without missions should come to an end.

Divine; please grant us leaders with mission as well as leaders with vision. Else, we would trample on our mission when we lack the vision to see it. Give us leaders who are capable of reconciling mad races and feuding faiths.

CHAPTER 10

▼

MAD RACES

Ours is a world of nuclear giants and ethical infants. We know more about wars than we know about peace, more about killing than we know about living. We have grasped the mystery of the atom and rejected the Sermon on the Mount.
—Omar Bradley

Brother KKK, what do you think about violence of the people by the people and for the people? It is the festering sore on mankind's conscience. Humans dwell in one world, but they lack one word for renouncing bigotry. We share one destiny, but we are short of an entity to banish intolerance. Six million Jews and several millions of other categories of people died in the wake of the Holocaust. Adolf Hitler, leader of the Third Reich, in his own wisdom, unleashed the pogrom that was the first of its kind in modern times. Mankind continued to advance in knowledge, but we did not advance in getting along. One expected man to have learned the biggest lesson in getting along, but the world has witnessed hundreds of grim wars and genocides since the Holocaust.

It has been wars without end. Millions are dead, and millions more are bereaved. Millions of civilians, children, and women have perished in wars they knew nothing about. Millions of displaced people have sought refuge far away from their homes and dignities. But mankind has yet to halt the intolerance of man by man. Military expenditure continues to skyrocket. Weapons of mass destruction are becoming stealthier and more destructive. Mankind is polluting the world, frying the earth he holds in trust for posterity with waste from nuclear reactors, chemicals, and biological weapons. Massive caches of weapons, tons of arms, and substantial amounts of land mines are in abundant supply around the world. Acts of terrorism are becoming sophisticated and deadlier than ever. Explosives used to explode on their own, but brainwashed, naïve, and suicidal youths now explode with them intentionally. Mankind's clock is ticking toward an apocalyptic midnight.

Can you see how wanton our world has become, Brother KKK? Nations are taking advantage of nations, profiting from lethal weapons sold to countries where millions of innocent children and women starve. Through underhanded loans, cutthroat repayment requests, imbalanced trade transactions, trade deficits, and unhealthy business practices, generous nations are offering aid to bankrupt nations and taking back what they offered in tenfold. Nations engage in systematic stealing from the poor by harboring the wealth stolen from pitiable nations. Multinational businesses are ripping off poor host nations via exploitative conditions, environmental degradation, unethical labor practices, tax evasion, harassment of native workers, and hazardous working conditions. Statistics show that one percent of rich people in the world are richer than more than half of the world population at the bottom of the economic ladder.

Many governments advocate goodwill for all, but they engage in double standards for all. Some advocate liberty, civil rights, sovereignty, and egalitarianism, but they lend a hand to dictatorial juntas when convenient. They even dine, wine, and trade with nations whose systems they condemned. Nations undermine governments elsewhere for refusing to offer natural resources; opposing business deals; and refusing to welcome military bases. Countries flaunt power. Their foreign policies emphasize that they've got the power. Manipulation and arm-twisting remain fair games. They see nothing wrong with influencing world politics and economies to their advantage. Nations are branding nations names that should be their own middle names.

Mindless leaders and government officials are fleecing their own people of their wealth, creating destitute children who should not starve. Leaders without vision and mission rob their own countries entirely, leaving millions of vulnerable children to die of malnutrition. They transfer stolen wealth to countries that do not even respect them. Millions of people are dying of preventable diseases each year, courtesy of shameless leaders misappropriating the wealth. Millions more are dying because they could not withstand the hardships associated with dwelling in slums. Embezzlement of wealth by people in charge of nations denies children, youths, and the elderly the basic things of life, including food, shelter, and clothing. Considerable amounts of children cannot go to school because their governments fund lousy official ceremonies in place of edification. Multitudes of children are denied education because they are females. No wonder, several centuries after formal education began, a large chunk of world population remains ignorant.

Countries are breeding fraudulent youths. Robbers are taking the place of the middle class, a consequence of the fallout from corruption and misplacement of priorities by graceless leaders. The beauty of democracy is not attractive to many because they have to survive first to participate in the government of the people by the people and for the people. Human rights are fairy tales to many because they need leaders with human faces first. Freedom of speech, press, and religion sound hollow to millions because they are not even free to fill their stomachs. Women remain devoted to their husbands and children despite the fact that they are denied so much. They do strenuous jobs for long hours, and they earn less than their male counterparts. But they cannot drive their own cars or visit friends by themselves in some countries. This should be a woman's world, too.

Children constitute large portions of some countries' militaries. Many nations do not see atrocious child labor as a problem. Child prostitution and pornography even thrive under the noses of leaders who tagged themselves as providing benevolent governance. Several centuries after the bell of freedom chimed in many countries, many children are not in a better condition than slaves are. Many do not see this as a problem because the inopportune kids belong to some poor folks in some unfortunate lands and climes. What went around could come around some day! Brain drain and human trafficking have taken the place of slavery, even though we thought that slave trade ended a while ago. Despotism is the real deal in some cultures. Dying in power is considered an achievement. Opposition leaders are periled and forbidden in many parts of the world.

I could imagine some nations' officials spewing anger from their ears, nostrils, and mouths already because someone is talking about the most guarded, yet open, secrets of the century. No nation has swum across the pool of integrity. No race has sprinted to the finishing line of goodness. All have withheld something and soiled their hands when they could have come to the table with clean hands. No group owns the cartel of immorality. No religion dominates the world of violence. All are guilty before divinity. Every nation is liable for pushing mankind to the edge. Every race has something to do to make the world a better place. All nations, races, religions, and groups owe the debt of remaking the world. No nations, kingdoms, or realms should hence christen others evil. All have sinned and come short before the judge of heaven and earth.

Brother KKK, I know you are fuming over all of these. I am, too. Now you can see why the world is going crazy. You now know why someone is mad at everyone and everybody is angry with somebody. You understand why the vicious circle of poverty refuses to go away in some parts of the world and the cruel circle of hatred refuses to break in others. Should I explain again why the vicious circle refuses to give the world a break? Nations engage the advantages so they have to cheat others. Some harbor stolen wealth from other countries. Many leaders rob their own people and mortgage the future of the coming generations to hopelessness. The vulnerable nations become poorer and more desperate. Children are starving, youths are unemployed, and women are helpless.

Jobless, insolvent, and lack of self-esteem males have no names to protect. They believe they have nothing to lose if they do stupid things. Their female counterparts have nothing to live for. Life has become a burden for them to bear. Many become rampaging bulls in the world's china shops. They see nothing wrong with the horrendous practice of swindling the citizens of wealthy nations because they rightly or wrongly perceive them as rip-offs. Are the swindlers justified for gouging an eye for an eye? Of course, they are not. He who justifies vice for a vice is vile. Evil practices have no other names than evil. Doing wrong to correct wrong does not right any wrong. Worse still, many of the broken youths could become tools of destruction in a fragile world. Remember that the devil finds jobs for idle hands.

Unemployed youths cherish good things of life, too. They live in a fast-moving world where one is on his own if he has nothing to be proud of. Frustrated youths become social miscreants and take to unspeakable activities. They deal drugs, commit armed robbery, engage in prostitution, commit suicide, assassinate others, encourage hatred, and engage in cruelty to humans and animals. These are just some of the dastardly results when the world generates demons out of naïve youths. The mother who says her child should not sleep has to stay awake to do so. The world that desires peace can no longer afford tranquility because deprived people are rumbling. Rich people can no longer sleep well at night because poor people are not in bed. Desolate and desperate nations are becoming havens and training grounds for extremists. They believe they have nothing to lose if their jobless youths become suicide bombers.

Do they have something to lose? They have everything to lose as they blow away their posterity agonizingly. The world is going crazy. What goes around is coming around. Somehow, the vicious circle of despondence is encircling both the rich and poor in a mad world.

Do I sound like a pessimist, Brother KKK? I am actually an optimist in a bewildered world. I am embracing reality, regardless of its price. I did not intend to be an apocalyptic prophet. I am interested in a sane world for our children. It is difficult to be factual in a world that estranges itself from facts. The truthful often become the deceitful. The pretender emerges as the candid one in an insincere world. He who says all is well when everything is not well becomes the hero. He who rings the bell of caution turns the villain. We listen to sweet nothings from politicians, but we deflect the harmless warning from the sages from our ears. The world dislikes reality. Maybe I am just saying that we all have some goodness in us and should bring out the good so the world could stop listing in an uncertain sea of self-destruction.

Brother KKK, our wild world is going crazy. Nations are blaming their woes on other nations. People are blaming their miseries on other people. Races are mad at other races. Religions are not pleased with other religions. Gangs are raging at other gangs. Mankind is mad at himself! Mutual Assured Destruction (MAD) is our lot if races remain mad at each other and people go nuts against one another everywhere. Mankind is mad at himself when races are mad at each other. Can we afford to be mad at one another when we have no known relatives in an endless universe? We are the world. We owe the debt of watching each other's back. We are the distant brothers who need no preachers to reconcile to one another. You are my brother. I am your brother, Brother KKK.

Arabs, Asians, blacks, Hispanics, Jews, Native Americans, Persians, Russians, whites, and the rest of the world cannot afford to make the planet an intolerable globe. All must unite. Christians, Muslims, Hindus, Buddhists, and Jews must learn tolerance. Kabbalah, Shintoism, Bahaism, Sikhism, Scientology, Zoroastrianism, and Unitarianism should be skilled at generating patience. Tolerance is love. Unity is progress. Diversity is beautiful. Intolerance is hatred. Disunity is retrogression. Loneliness is friendlessness. Tolerance, unity, and diversity are for good. Intolerance, disunity, and loneliness are for evil. Races should stop raging against each other. People must stop hating one another.

Man continues to go through the well-known circle of adversity throughout history without coming to a close. The familiar loop of misfortune persists as humans search for influence over others. People think about themselves so much without reflecting on the vicious ring. The furious sphere of misfortune refuses to go away. Many feel better about themselves when others linger below them. Leaders tackle the fiery, circular misfortune with talks so the world could see them in action. They convene more and more talks without affirmative resolutions. They sometimes figure out how to tame the recurring hard times, but they lack the audacity to follow through. The vicious circle continues. More talks follow.

Mankind's fiery ferry smothers on a troubled sea of self-destruction as stunned men, women, and children watch. People express fresh horrors as new waves of wars, genocides, terrorism, and violence of the people by the people and for the people ravage the planet. As usual, international media revisit the historical frenzy of agitating people with up-to-the-minute reports whenever new carnages unfurl. Overwhelmed citizens of the world, which conscientious nongovernmental organizations lead, become outraged once again. They remind leaders about their sworn promises to make the world a better place for all. The leaders gather once again and engage in more talks. They return to the solutions that are hardly ever pursued. Everyone is reassured once again. Nobody stops the vicious circle thereafter. The world waits in oblivion until another season of violence unfolds.

I cannot say there are aliens from other planets, but an unexpected raid by an armada of UFOs may not differentiate between races, colors, national boundaries, and languages. If they exist, alien crewmembers may disregard worldly borders. They may not distinguish between the diverse religions before taking prisoners of war with them. Asteroids would create craters wherever they would land without differentiating between nations and cultures. Natural disasters do not draw any boundaries between races or colors. Global warming, tsunamis, hurricanes, thunderstorms, volcanic eruptions, wildfires, and diseases do not discriminate between races and colors. We share one planet and a borderless air space that lacks curtains. Why can't we just unite and protect our planet? Why can't we all just get along and stop the world from going crazy? Time is running out for the mad races in a crazy world.

Hear me out, Brother KKK. You and I should be on the same page when it comes to saving our world from sliding down the perilous cliff of intolerance. If we do not refrain from hurting one another, races would send other races to the guillotine. If we fail to unite, people would be crucifying other people.

Can mankind afford to hang himself? Why are nations holding the keys to the pillories and stocks that hold one another down without lifting a hand? Should we watch as man lowers the ducking stool that holds man into the shark-invested sea of uncertainty? What would mankind get for sending himself to the gallows? How long would man continue to crack the cruel whip of hatred on man?

The world needs new heroes. We want fresh heroines. We want daring women who are not scared of meeting intolerance on a single-lane bridge. We want valiant men and courageous women who are not fearful when standing by what is neither secure nor fashionable. Simply, their sense of right and wrong says it is right. Mankind needs everyday heroes who put smiles on people's faces everywhere. Our new heroes may lack the ability to jump from high-rise buildings, but they can wipe tears from the victims of hate crimes. The fresh heroines may be short of skills to leap from fast-moving vehicles, but they can advocate tolerance. The world needs help. We need brave men and women who are not scared of promoting charity. We want patient youths who tolerate other races, cultures, and groups.

Can you hear the lone voice from the backwoods urging hatred to depart?

"Go away from our world, prejudice!" hollers the voice. "Racism must flee. Ignorance must leave. Bigotry must retreat."

Listen to the sage's voice, Brother KKK. The oracle has no reason to lie. Man's clock ticks toward apocalyptic midnight as the watchers in the fortress slumber. Someone must wake up the leaders. Man must mend his ways before divinity charts a new course for mankind. We make the world an uncertain planet, but we wonder why man cannot tolerate man. We marvel at why the world continues to drift in an endless space of dilemma. Man destroys his homestead with intolerance as brothers fight over skin colors. Peoples fight over religions as they edge love out of their places of worship.

Radical preachers advocate hatred in churches, mosques, shrines, and synagogues. Innocent children die as a result. Christians, Jews, and Muslims think about what separates them more than what unites them. Brothers despise brothers. Sons of the same father continue to injure one another. Can't Abraham's children listen to what the sage is saying in the grave?

"Unity, peace, and love! Patience, mercy, and forgiveness!" hollers the voice from the grave.

Harmony, compassion, and prayer, not agony, abrasion, or slayer, wins the hearts and souls of men. Man should be desperate for kindness if he is desperate. He should be anxious for agreement among mankind if he is anxious. We have choices to make. Our destinies lie in our hands.

We determine our fate. We are the architects of our fortune. Heaven only helps those who help themselves. The healing of human injuries begins with acts of tolerance from man to man. Mankind determines his bill of health. The Divine only heals those who accept his prescriptions. Be a hero, Brother KKK. Make heroes out of your sons. Turn into an idol. Create idols from your daughters. The world needs heroes and idols that fashion tolerance from intolerance, healing from hurting, and conviction from suspicion. The centuries of mistrust among humans did not bring glory to mankind. The acrimony that religions shared over the years has no splendor. Nothing good comes from man's animosity to man. It is time for a change.

A rainstorm pronounces its coming to the blind with a rumbling windstorm. It announces its coming to the deaf with deep clouds. I could hear the echoing whirlwind. The dark clouds are thick enough to warn man about the approaching rain. A deluge of rain awaits mankind if the world runs short of heroes. We need heroes who transcend races in their thoughts. We want heroines who rise above skin colors in their deeds. We need faithful who go beyond flaunting religions, but they show kindness, forgiveness, and healing to fellow humans. The world needs unfaltering children. They are the hope of tomorrow and trustees of a peaceful future. Else, nature would be mad at man for centuries of abuse and ingratitude. Grant us heroes, Divine. Give us heroines, providence.

Brother KKK, I could feel Mother Nature reprimanding man for thwarting diversity. The signs of the time are authenticating nature's resentment against man's abuse of her gifts. Grounds are soaked everywhere. The spilled blood of breadwinners is being rejected. Mother Earth is disheartened and weary of interning innocent boys that the malnutrition commissioned by greedy leaders killed. She can no longer confine the bodies of innocent girls killed by land mines sold by leaders that place riches first. How could man be sleepy and miss the signs that the disappointed Mother Nature revealed? Where are the leaders? Where are the heroes? Mankind snores as disenchanted nature gives signs far and wide, especially in the sky, on land, in the water, and everywhere.

Global warming threatens the future generations of children as leaders watch businesses pillage the environment. Beware of the ominous signs of the time! What more signs are we waiting for? Fields are heavily contaminated with chemicals. Challenging diseases are bringing innocent children on their knees. Minefields are not disappearing. But leaders whose countries manufacture and distribute mines preach peace. Teeming forests are disappearing and giving way to bare lands. Nonetheless, nations that plunder the environment are going very slow about going green. Mountains of ice are disappearing from the North Pole to the South Pole. Avalanches, landslides, mudslides, and erosions are overwhelming our earth. Unprecedented flooding is overtaking our cities. Deserts are becoming hotter. Man's extreme weather vocabularies are expanding, including tsunami, La Niña, El Niño, and more. Heed the signs of the time. Mother Nature is going mad, too.

Man takes diversity for granted. He grunts at varieties and the multiplicity of men, women, and children on the surface of earth. Imagine how glad the lonely astronauts are every time visiting astronauts arrive at the International Space Station. Circumstances make them appreciate fellow humans, but men on the ground take the diverse population of people for granted everywhere. It takes the orphan who looks up to the sun as father to appreciate fathers. It takes the lonely child who watches the moon as mother to value mothers. It takes the street urchin who counts on stars as relatives to understand the gift of family. But unap-

preciative peoples look down on one another when they should be compliment-
ing and complementing each other.

Brother KKK, can you hear the voiceless people that barefaced racism injured
around the world? The cold hands of bias have tormented innocent children,
women, and men. Can you see the lethargic silhouettes made of people that the
pretentious sun of inequality illuminated? Humans are engaging in inhumane
acts against other humans. Can't you smell the sulfur emanating from hell called
prejudice? It is the obnoxious whiff of disparity from hell. You should be concerned about how man victimizes other men on earth. Would you stand and
watch as man fights his own shadow? I am concerned about how brothers perse-
cute their brothers. Man is mad at man. Mother Nature is mad at man. So far,
man has carried himself in a world where mankind is his own enemy.

We now understand why the world is crazy. It is now implicit why races are
mad at other races. It is no longer hidden why people are angry with other people. You now know why nations are irritated by other nations. I am now aware
why gangs fume at other gangs. Wait a minute, Brother KKK. Should the mad-
ness tarry forever? Must we jeopardize the future generations of mankind? Can
wars without end bring harmony to the world? Would the coming generations
know peace if they would inherit a brutally divided planet? Can the world be any
better without man forgiving himself? Uncountable are the wrongs by man
against other men. It is so many that every man could have a bagful to himself.
But many wrongs would not make a right if two wrongs could not make a right.

We are still here because man tried to right some of the wrongs by man against
man. The world remains because the beast in man develops a human face sometimes. The promise of a better future becomes clearer as man regains sanity.

What would have become of the world if slavery had endured? Would civilization have thrived if segregation remained as ugly as it was? Could the world have
survived by tolerating every Hitler that manifested? How much of cooperation
would have existed among mankind if the world had failed to isolate terrorism as
a beast that lacked goodwill for all? What would have become of the earth if man
had not evolved beyond the level of real dogs eating dogs in the street? Our beautiful globe would have become a well-stocked terracotta shop with rampaging
bulls.

What if we take the righting of wrongs to the next level? Healing starts with an
admission of wrongdoing for letting each other down. Consenting social justice,
mutual respect, and tolerance to roam the world freely is a great idea. Maybe
returning what we wrongly took from one another would melt hardened hearts.
Then clemency would flow like a river from the mountain. People would be

compassionate to people. Cultures would grant amnesty to cultures. Nations would exonerate nations. Governments would pardon governments. Religions would endure religions. Faithful would tolerate nonbelievers. Listen to the voice from the mountain. Heed the signs of the time as nature protests man's abuses. Let justice flow from high places and drown injustices at low places. Prevent Mutual Assured Destruction from obliterating the races.

CHAPTER 11

▼

LIVING PHANTOM

Do all the good you can, by all the means you can, in all the ways you can, in all the places you can, at all the times you can, to all the people you can, as long as ever you can.
—John Wesley

Brother KKK, do you mind if I tell you another story about people who were mad at people? One octogenarian neighbor did not have any good words for those who looked different from him. Through other people, I heard he had called me a racial name for no apparent reason. I decided to confront him in a forward-thinking manner. Instead of emitting anger from my nostrils, I spoke to the man like a friend. He was surprised that I pushed love to him after he shoved hatred to me. It was unusual after all to receive fish from the people we gave snake. The elderly man looked remorseful. Against our other neighbors' expectation of witnessing two gladiators generating unprecedented turmoil in the neighborhood, we became friends. The scuttlebutt who reported the old man to me earlier even became jealous.

My old friend had nothing except good words to say about other people for a long time. I thought I had finally succeeded in kicking racism, one at a time, out of some people. But I felt terrible when my friend uttered fresh racial slurs against a neighbor who belonged to another race. It was the first time in a long time. He uttered the words involuntarily before realizing what he said. He was unusually sad that he expressed those hurtful words in my presence. Clearly, he wished he had not said what came out of his mouth. Mine was double agony. I was not pleased with what he said and the fact that those words came out of his mouth. I held a strong heart-to-heart talk with my friend there and then. The sobered man admitted he needed to revise his ways of life like he never did.

My aged neighbor and friend was not the only one who had a reason to look at the world differently. I did, too. Every one of us needed to. I cast my pride aside and pitied my frailty and those of fellow human beings. I realized how flimsy and inferior we were when we assumed that we were better than others. The stark imperfection of a prejudiced mind worried me. I was sad about the narcissism that we embraced as a living species. I wondered what business the man who probably only had a few years left had to do with prejudice. I expected my aged friend to be persistent with correcting the errors he made in the early parts of his life. I anticipated he would be concerned with building bridges among peoples and cultures so he could leave the world better than he met it. I guessed he should be enhancing the world with love in his last years so his children would inherit a commonsensical world.

I felt sad by the defenselessness of mankind as we subjected ourselves to the outlandish flight of our imaginations. The ridiculous fantasy that man bred as he behaved like he would live forever distressed me. Imagine a man who could go to bed one night without waking up the following morning drenching himself with prejudice toward people that did not look like him.

How could someone who witnessed the carnage that trailed the Holocaust contemplate prejudice ever again? Why did the man who should have the wisdom of Solomon and shrewdness of Jacob allow pettiness to consume him? How could the man who should be an alpha and omega of worldly experiences become an ordinary thinker? How could the initiated act like an uninitiated?

There are thousands of reasons why no man should hate, Brother KKK. I have uncountable reasons why nobody should bear the world on his chest mischievously. Else, he would depart unsung by his own fault. I know why man should not detest fellow men. Consider the fact that man's years on earth are like a speck in an endless space of time. Man comes and goes too soon, like a candle caught in a windstorm. He does not have sufficient time to embrace land, wealth, and position. Man is endowed with barely enough years for etching honor on his name before returning to the soil. He lacks the luxury of living dishonorably for so long and retaining enough time to right the wrongs he generated. The world is for men, women, and children who know how to play the game of live and let live.

I have witnessed enough of the reasons why man should not carry the world selfishly in his baggage. We dwell in a world where man could own a bag of wealth in the morning and sleep with a bag of debt in the night. Many wake up from their own houses in the morning and share rooms with unintended neighbors at night after losing their treasured abodes. This is a world where a well-off, but mean, fellow could survive at the mercy of the nerd he mistreated a long time ago. It is not smart for a man to assume he owns the world when all he possesses is an illusion called wealth. Power is as transient as a tower of sand at the lower end of a rampaging river. The fleeting years of man are only good for sowing goodwill for the uncountable years that follow his demise. Haters depart and leave nothing except the eternal infamy attached to the aprons of mean fellows.

The very old ones among us would spend one hundred twenty years before departing the stage for newer generations. Many dwell for eighty years and leave. A lot of good people even head off when they are not ready to go. The honor they leave behind is the only thing that lives after them.

Why should man bear the world on his head, hating on the basis of race, when no race needs anyone to hate on its behalf? Why does man hurt others on the basis of skin color when he would soon relinquish the skin to Mother Earth? Why do religious people detest others on the basis of faith when honoring the Divine and his creations should be the duty of the faithful?

I know more reasons why man should not quench his thirst with the mirage called racial pride instead of the living water called love. It is okay to celebrate one's race, but no one elevates his race by lowering other races.

Brother KKK, I am aware that the road of life is not an endless boulevard. It is a blind alley for those who generate malice in place of goodwill. They live and depart without leaving something constructive behind. How clever is the man who generates malice on his way out when he may lack the opportunity to return and right the wrongs he created? I am not interested in writing you a missive of fear, Brother KKK. But everything herein is a possibility. Quite a few people from the four corners of the world depart daily without the chance to bid loved ones good-bye. Afterward, why does man hold onto what belongs to nature as if it belongs to him forever? It has never been—and would never be—for mortal man to own the wide world to himself. Man owns the world with goodwill, not ill will.

Never ever say never. Do not look down on others because you are fortunate. No living man lives on an island of invulnerability. Vulnerability does not respect any mortal being. No one has the association of poverty. The man who wakes up vulnerable in the morning could get lucky by bedtime. Wealth has no permanent friends. Poverty has no lasting enemies. Monarchs lose their royalties sometimes. Street urchins find themselves at high places occasionally. Hard work is unquestionably the remedy against poverty, but life sometimes turns to a bridge without guardrails on a shark-infested ocean. The hard-working man should not even look down on others because he cannot tell what tomorrow will bring. Wherever a man finds himself, therefore, let him ally himself with goodwill, charity, and humility.

Whoever walks at high places should not christen fellow men with preposterous names. Abstain from making life miserable for others when you tread the corridor of power. Authority sometimes strips man naked without him knowing. How a man relates to fellow men determines how far his home is from honor or dishonor. He who builds fountains of hope in his lifetime rests in lush meadows of admiration in death. Whoever creates a wilderness of despair in his lifetime sleeps in a blistering backwoods of repulsion in death. People do not celebrate those who estrange themselves to benevolence before departing the world. Only the wise maintains respect and tolerance for fellow men. Understanding the futility of hatred belongs to the clever among men. Hatemonger lives and dies miserably as the melancholic spirit of hatred breeds nothing except misery. Mean people become the harshest parts of people's hearts. Benevolent people live at the paramount corner of hearts. Compassionate people live and die happily as the happiness they randomly throw around mob them everywhere they go.

Am I sounding pessimistic enough, Brother KKK? I guarantee that I have nothing in common with pessimism and I live far away from glumness. I do not share common grounds with cynicism. I am only saying that man cannot plant an ear of hatred and reap a bouquet of love in return. I am articulating the fact that life, for any reason, is not worth hating people for. Man owns land for eighty years, but land owns man forever as he enters his last place of rest. Therefore, why should man hate fellow men because of land? Wealth sometimes turns its back on friends. Bankruptcy occasionally walks into the lives of strangers.

Why should anyone detest others because of short-lived fortune? Why do people look down on others because of skin color, religion, and class? The world is not the right planet for hating fellow humans.

Are you with me, Brother KKK? Man may have ideas, but no one can definitely say what tomorrow holds. Let he who knows what tomorrow holds in stock for man come out and tell. No mortal, except the benevolent who plants goodwill all over the world, could predict his ultimate end. The world moves, and man follows as he refuses to take the lead and direct the world responsibly. He who has ears should hear. He who has eyes should see the futility of bearing the ogre called hatred on his chest. Let the bird who nests at home hear and communicate with the ones in the wilderness that it takes the shrewd to love and the tactless to hate.

The dog that would get lost does not listen to its master's whistle. Fate overloads people with pride when it wants them to get lost, so they will not ask for direction or seek wise counsel. Such people lack respect for fellow humans and see nothing good in other people. They are oblivious to the fact that nature created nothing that was useless. Inordinate pride is the beginning of a headlong descent into the abyss of disgrace. Respect for others only takes nothing except dishonor away from anyone. Reverence for fellow humans comes after the veneration for the Divine. Regrettably, many assign more value to exotic bugs than fellow humans. They offer greater comfort to pets than fellow humans. They give dogs colorful names and christen fellow men with derogatory nomenclatures.

The world exists with contrasting creatures for a reason, specifically young and old, male and female, rich and poor, black and white, religious and atheist, and so forth. I guess they are here to complement one another. There is no way to compare one thing and another if they are not different. We know that something is hot because another thing is cold. We understand that someone is rich because someone else is poor. Diverse things complement each other. It is not the responsibility of the fortunate man to look down on the poor. It is his responsibility to complement them. He is well-off so he can count his blessings, name them one by one, and be appreciative of life. The well-to-do man is not done yet until he engages the leverage of prosperity to make the world a better place, not worse.

Bless you, Brother KKK, if you are following me. I did not intend to tie you down with a lengthy mail, but this is undoubtedly a perceptibly indispensable epistle. You are aware that brothers are free to communicate judiciously with each other. What happens to the love and respect we have for one another if we do not commune? Brothers are there with shoulders that are large enough for one another to rest when necessary. They listen to one another's thrills and drills. I am thrilled that I can communicate with you whenever I want. You are my only nature-given cohort on the mysterious and arduous road of life. Imagine how dreary and troublesome life would be without a brother and a friend to chat with. Please tolerate my elongated missive of love.

That is enough of intentional digression. Else, we would unintentionally digress from the heart of this distinctive letter. Let's revisit the reasons why prejudice is no longer as hot as it used to be. The art and science of looking down on others now belong to the shortsighted. Farsighted individuals have looked across the distanced road of hatred, but they did not see anything honorable. Hence, analytical and discerning minds gave up on the fruitless endeavor of discrimination a while ago. Rational minds everywhere are now tinkering with the scheme of building a universal civilization of tolerance. An inclusive culture of acceptance where no man is inferior is in the making. Every man is coming to the table with an open mind. Every woman is coming to the table with open hands. There are spacious places for you and me to rebuild the world.

Lobbing politically incorrect slurs is no longer politically correct. The gathering of decent no longer defends the indefensible. People now get into trouble for using their heads for hateful endeavors more than they use them for reasoning. All are welcome to the participatory world of tolerance where vanquished is now an outdated vocabulary. Race, religion, and association no longer decide where people sit. Instead, the aggregate of efforts to build a better world determine people's positions. Again, no one is superior. No one is inferior. Different folks possess unique gifts. Man brings his talent to the table. Woman comes with her endowment. Grown people throw their gifts to the table. Children chip in their flairs. Whoever thinks that some groups of people have little to offer in the partnership of making the world a better place should listen to the story of what the young does better than the grown-ups.

Once upon a time, the ancient town of *All's Worthy* became stuck. The people no longer made progress because they allowed hostility to creep into their community. Somebody was mad at something. Everything offended everybody. There were enough reasons for people to be angry with other people. The community leaders were sectional. They thought only about their families and friends alone. The judges made justice too expensive for ordinary people to purchase. As if things were not bad enough, the elite started counseling their children against associating with commoners. Segregation started rearing its ugly head. It was an epoch of revolt. Animosity camped everywhere. More than ever, people began to detest one another. Everything was spinning out of control. Things were so bad that religious leaders, the formerly last hope for peace, started preaching hatred. In this era, everything went wrong for one town.

The diverse faiths began to undercut one another. People started misquoting the scriptures. The faithful were using the verses to enhance their personal agenda. Children who once used to have several diverse friends started restricting themselves to the members of their groups. People began to look down on one another. Every group was on the edge. People from different social backgrounds demoralized each other. Sabotage became the biggest challenge to the town's landmarks as milestones of civilization were under severe threat. Everyone had something to worry about. Nobody was free from the fallouts of hardships that the general animosity brought. Never had a community had so much pain like the town of *All's Worthy*.

The council of elders understood that they had to do something swift. Else, the formerly serene and progressive town would become history. They invited the town's oracle and instructed him to consult with the Divine so the town could regain its sanity. The aged seer slowly walked into the town hall and set to work. Much to the chagrin of people who were used to eloquent and sweet-talking politicians, he spoke at his convenience.

"Listen to the ramblings of a sage. Pay little attention to the eloquence of politicians," cautioned the small man. He switched to an unfamiliar tune shortly. "Peace was not scarce during Olugbon's time. Dearth of harmony was missing in Aresa's era. Justice was ten for a penny when Lamurin lived. What has gone wrong since our father's time? Ela, the peaceful one, climb down on our town. Man is self-destructing. Tranquility is fading. Climb down, Ela, the judicious knight."

The oracle appeased the Divine and asked for peace in the town of *All's Worthy*. Everywhere was so silent that one could almost hear a pin drop. Everyone knew why the town degenerated so fast, but they wanted to know what would bring the community back to her feet.

"Living phantom!" began the old oracle. "Man holds life to his chest needlessly and hallucinates about living forever. People disrespect one another unnecessarily. Once a bosom friend, peace is now a stranger to *All's Worthy* because man feeds on ego and thrives on vanity."

He reported the Divine's message to his people, "Allow prejudice to shrivel and permit patience to blossom. Stop looking down on one another. Enthrone unity as the guiding principle of the community. Then *All's Worthy* would be on her feet in no time."

He could hear the voice of the Divine when others appeared deaf to the dire warnings of the great one. The old man revealed the Divine would raise *All's Worthy* back to her feet, but the town had to undergo a test.

"Inclusive existence, where nobody is left behind or besmirched, is the vehicle for unity," emphasized the old man.

The Divine was patient. He forgave the stubborn people of *All's Worthy*, but he wanted to teach them a lesson in humility. It was not strange that arrogance was the culprit for the people's culture of looking down on one another. Thus, he wanted them to understand that looking down on others was not a shrewd endeavor.

The Divine was determined to feed the people of *All's Worthy* with humble pies. Thus, he highlighted the test they would undergo through the oracle. The great one instructed that he would leave pieces of unity marbles on the shelf in the town's treasure room. Another pack would be in a gourd on the floor below the shelf.

"There would be unity, peace, and progress once you are able to piece the two sets of unity marbles together," instructed the matured seer. "One more thing … bare hands. No ladder. No picking devices. Man cannot use his manipulative contrivances this time. Again, you must not turn the gourds upside down."

"Piece of cake," assured the town's mayor. "Go home everyone. Come back in the morning so we can piece together the Divine's marbles of unity."

The pride that brought the people of *All's Worthy* to their knees had not departed. They all went home, thinking they had a simple task ahead of them. None of the people understood that the Divine sometimes tested people for humility in little ways imaginable. They equated the great one's thoughts to man's thoughts. They reduced his principles to the mechanical principles of the machines that man used for manipulating the environment. The test was uncomplicated, but the Divine intended to educate man with the twist that came with it. He wanted no man to impose himself on others, regardless of his place.

The people of *All's Worthy* could not wait for the next day to break. They gathered at the town hall before dawn. As usual, the council of elders took the lead in opening the treasure room. There was no democracy. The elders were at liberty to do all things the way they deemed on behalf of the town. The Divine was watching from above and waiting to see how the people would piece together the marbles of unity. The elders lifted their hands and reached for the marbles on the shelf. That was easy. Then it was time to retrieve the ones from the gourds on the ground. The elders stooped on their knees and grabbed the gourds, trying to force their hands inside. Unfortunately, their hands were too big to enter the tiny openings. They understood the instructions that they could not use anything except bare hands to retrieve the marbles. They also remembered they could not turn the gourds upside down.

The elders labored stubbornly to get the marbles out of the gourds. The Divine laughed himself silly. A group of people believed they owned the patents to all activities in the town. Thank goodness! The oracle was around to save the day. He instructed the elders to step aside.

"You did your part correctly by retrieving the marbles from the shelf. Now recognize what another group has to offer," he asked as he opened the door and allowed a group of kids to walk into the treasure room.

It only took the minors a fraction of the time that the elders labored to no avail to retrieve the marbles from the gourds. The kids slipped their tiny hands into the gourds and brought out all of the marbles without hassles.

"The town of *All's Worthy* was built on the conjecture that elders were shrewd and the young were smart," tutored the oracle.

It was time for him to walk the people of *All's Worthy* through the lesson of humility that the Divine intended to teach the people.

"The world was predicated on the principle that the diverse groups had to complement and compliment one another to the advantage of all," explained the aged diviner as he looked at the embarrassed council of elders.

He further clarified to the people of *All's Worthy*, who were elated there would be unity, peace, and progress after all, regardless of who retrieved the marbles from where. "No one should pride himself with being better than others. It does not matter if a man spots the snake and a woman puts it away. It only matters as long as the poisonous creature does not hurt defenseless children."

You can see the logic behind the Divine's modest test for the people of *All's Worthy*, Brother KKK. Children's hands cannot reach the shelf because they were not long enough. The adults' hands could not enter the gourds because they were too big. No one would have sweated if the two groups had understood their individual shortcomings and came together to achieve their joint goal. The town of *All's Worthy* is a microcosm of the world we live in. It is rare to find someone who has it all. Diverse folks have diverse talents. The world could be a little better if the diverse folks compliment and complement one another, as Mother Nature intended.

Regrettably, man cannot read between the lines as Mother Nature endowed the diverse regions of the world diversely. International trade exists because no nation has it all. Countries exchange their diverse goods for that purpose. Why can't man relate to that logic, work together as partners, and move mankind forward jointly? Remember, no group has yet to establish a separate planet somewhere in the dark space apart from this weary world. We have two choices ahead of us. Mankind could stick together and survive together. Or we could continue with the senseless war of attrition. We could exploit the universal brotherhood of man to mankind's advantage. Or brothers could continue to hate brothers senselessly. Man could remain so advanced, but so backward.

Great is the loss of the man kicked out by a member of his group, but rejects the welcoming gesture of a member of another group on the ground that they do not belong to the same group. Nobody should reject the friendship of other peoples because they are not members of his race. Rejecting harmless people on the basis of their skin color is unwise. Whoever judges a man by the color of his skin, not the contents of his character, is a master of mischief. By no means would a man please an all-loving God by spilling the blood of defenseless children. The man who hurts others on the basis of difference in association is the loser of all time. We brought nothing here. We will depart with nothing. The jewelry that enters the ground with a dead man belongs to the worms. Nature created nothing that was useless. Everyone is worthy. Maybe *All's Worthy* should be the world's first name. It is time to coexist responsibly when one group cannot send the other to another planet. Current generations of mankind have nothing to lose by becoming good shepherds to the flock that follows.

CHAPTER 12

▼

VALIANT SHEPHERD

The test of the morality of a society is what it does with its children.
—Dietrich Bonhoeffer

Brother KKK, I have more words yearning for listeners. Thoughtful elders passed these insightful words on to me. These words do not fail to come to pass. They happen by dinnertime if they do not come to pass at the breakfast table. Please pay attention to my words once again. It takes the astute to listen to wise counsel and the shrewd to embrace logical reasoning. The smart man walks away from emotion and stands by actuality. The ignorant pitches his tent anywhere that sentiment drives him. Sadly, the ignorant is not aware of his predicament most of the time. I pray, my brother, that you would give a wide berth to emotion. We must stay away from sentiment now that we have come of age. Else, the younger generations would notice how sentiment ruled us. Now let's go on another voyage of using words to remake the world.

Little venomous snakes take after their parents in the business of biting to kill. Scorpions raise their young ones for injuring people. Black widows nurture their babies so they could exterminate victims. Multitudes of red ants discover the act of biting from their parents. Little bees grow up to sting like their mothers. Stinging wasps learn how to hurt from their adults. A cobra's young ones do not look any bit like dove's hatchlings. A tiger's cubs resemble tigers only. Wolves train their children to rob shepherds of their sheep. Vultures rear their babies to deplete hens' chicks. The mother deer teaches her babies how to run and escape. A lioness raises the future carnivores of the savannah. Cubs take after tigers. Human children take after their parents.

Bees sting, but they become the most useful insects at some points in time. Once the most delicate insects, bees add sweetness to their character by giving honey to mankind. Once a pack of deadly insects in the wild, bees add colors to their temperament by pollinating and aiding the production of the most beautiful flowers around the world. What would flowers do without the pollinating bees? Nature is not all about stinging and harming. It is about sweetness and beauty at the right time. Unquestionably, humans have something to learn from bees. We should not remain spiteful creatures if hurtful insects know when to stop injuring. We should start making life sweet and beautiful. Mankind prides himself with being the higher animal, that is, the thoughtful being. Man has nothing to show for his pride if he is all about hurting and inflicting pain on fellow men. His cities cannot differentiate themselves from the wild, where only the fierce and untamed survives.

Brother KKK, I am glad that the world has a few men and women left who do not generate pains for others. I am thrilled that the planet has some conscientious people left. It is my pleasure that we have people who continue to engender charity for mankind. I am talking about men and women who do not limit goodwill to those who look like them. They initiate their young ones into spreading charity across the board. I am happy for those who refuse to teach their children hatred. It is my pleasure to recognize parents who discourage their children from discriminating. I am proud of fathers who do not pass on the art of extermination to their sons. The mothers who restrain their daughters from hating deserve rounds of applause. I have utmost respect for parents who teach love to their children.

What do you teach your children, Brother KKK? What do I teach my children? Do we teach our children how to sting like bees? Or do we teach them how to produce honey for all of mankind? Do they hurt with their mouths? Or do they pollinate the world with uniting words? Are we investing in the business of biting to kill, like venomous snakes? Have you been tutoring your children how to slander? Or have I been teaching mine how to malign? Do we school our young ones in the art of defaming those who are different? Are we nurturing black widows or little cupids? Have we been raising multitudes of red ants instead of comforting modest ones? Stinging bees, fierce wasps, noxious cobra, pilfering wolves, and precarious vultures are not practical models for human children.

Let's pour all that man lives for on the ground and pick them again ... one at a time. It will do well to select the meaningful things first rather than choosing the flimsy ones first. Nobody places the cart before the horse. Something is wrong when a man places dishonor before honor. Everything is wrong when a man considers hatred before tolerance. Racists place race before mankind and limit their horizons. Bigots place religion before love when mankind should celebrate love as the only religion known to man. Cowards eliminate fellow humans in the name of gangs because they lack the ingenuity to resolve issues without violence. Man results to aggression because he places edginess before patience and confrontation before diplomacy.

May I ask again, Brother KKK, what kind of father are you? I could imagine you asking me the same question. How reliable is the father who shows pieces of rocks to his child as loaves of bread because he wants to sell his thought to the poor child at all cost? How manly is it when a man brandishes lies as the truth in the presence of his young ones because he wants them to accept his doctrine? Is it honorable for a woman to celebrate bigotry in place of tolerance because she detests other people? Should mothers paint revulsion as love because they hate to see their children embrace people who are different from them? I am not afraid to say that something is wrong with whoever advocates hatred as an honorable thing because he hates others.

It is not a hypothesis that man would lie in his bed as he lays it. I know it is real that everyone shall reap whatever he sows in the world. He who disseminates hatred shall harvest repulsion. The man who spreads unity would die a hero. The one who propagates disunity would die unsung. You are responsible for the deception you tell your kids as the truth. I am liable for the ruse I sell to my children as facts. The father has the body, spirit, and soul of his child in his hands when the latter is young and naïve. Innocent children are mare clay in the hands of their mothers. We are responsible for what we mold out of our children. I am sure you did not hear the story of the thieving mother who taught her child how to thrive on pilfering.

Daka was a child with a difference. He started developing burly muscles at a tender age. Everyone respected him for his raw power. Unlike his contemporaries, he could run tedious errands without complaining. Everything about him called attention to his strong features. He could have become a celebrated wrestler, boxer, weight lifter, or something worthwhile later in his life. He had all it took to become famous, but it appeared like fate and his mother conspired to make him something else. Daka's mother thought what was good for her should be good for her son. She saw nothing wrong with her son learning and embracing what she held close to her chest. She did not mind teaching her son how to pilfer because she did not see anything wrong with it.

The woman passed on the idea of stealing to her child by making suggestive statements whenever they went to the marketplace. The boy witnessed his mother ingeniously wrapping little pieces of cow skin into her wrapper at the market without paying for them. "Is it okay to take what belongs to poor people without feeling guilty," asked the poor boy. "That's just fine," replied the immoral mother. Do you think the parent has the physical custody of the child alone? Think again. Symbolically, she has his soul and spirit as well. The child liberates his body, soul, and spirit from his parents only when he is old enough to choose his own way. Daka innocently embraced his mother's perverted way of life, believing that one is clever when he steals without the owner knowing. But he becomes a thief only when he is caught.

The poor boy would steal his peers' pencils and teachers' pens without a word of reproach from his mother. He realized that something was wrong with what he was doing, but he innocently assumed that he was helping himself in an unfair world. He knew nothing different from what his mother taught him. Daka perfected the art of stealing on a daily basis. It became the only act he knew how to perform without error. He could remove a wallet from the pocket of a tight-fitting pair of trousers without the owner noticing anything unusual about the innocent boy standing next to him. Daka was very good at what his mother taught him. Everyone, except his unrepentant mother, knew him as a crafty thief. He was the best child a pilfering mother could have.

Stealing so engrossed Daka that it was too late for him to rediscover himself. The boy graduated from picking pockets and shoplifting to raiding houses and shops. He soon became a creepy armed robber. Every endeavor has its own limit as man is bound to render accounts of his doings someday, somewhere, and somehow. Time was running out for Daka, but his mother, who taught him how to make life miserable for other people, could not stop him from plunging into the precipice of ignominy. No one looks perfect in human garb. Blunder has no master as the cleverest humans make mistakes, too. The thief celebrates his feat everyday, but the victim celebrates justice just one day, that is, the day the crook makes a mistake. Daka was about to make the mistake of his life. Every crafty criminal assumes he would go free until he finds his hands in handcuffs.

Unfortunately, Daka was arrested for armed robbery in a country where the crime carried the supreme penalty. He could not save himself. His mother could not lift a finger to protect her precious son any longer. It was too late for redemption. Daka's mother could only cry. People cherish what they have more when they are about to lose them. Owners discovered the hidden values of their belongings when they no longer have them. She was about to lose the child she believed would steal from others to take care of her when she was old. Robbery has never been an honorable business because robbers sometimes go out without returning home. Deceit may run for twenty years, but truth catches up with it in a day. The twist in Daka's story should dissuade parents who teach their children evil without thinking about the return of nature's revenge.

The judgment day came after months of judicial tango. Daka received the result of years of depriving people of their possessions.

"The court finds you guilty. You shall die by public execution," pronounced the judge somberly.

Daka was a hardened man. He did not show any emotion as the judge continued with the ceremonial admonition. "Do you have a request, Mr. Daka?" the judge asked if he had a last word. "May I talk to my mother, please," requested the criminal. "I see no reason why you should not speak with your mother," replied the judge. Daka made one more request as the judge asked him to speak. "Can I speak to her privately?" he asked. The judge granted the woman the chance to approach his shackled son. Then something nasty happened! As an act of revenge, Daka bit off his mother's ear.

"Why this lack of remorse at this period of your life?" asked the stunned and probing judge.

Daka appeared at ease as he told the court the story of how his mother ruined his life by raising him as a baby thief and later a heartless robber. The people in the courtroom looked at the next person as if they were all asking if they had been raising their children in some untraditional ways. The silence in the court, other than people's curious stares, was solid. Nobody expected what Daka did to his mother, but everyone understood why he did it. The whole event was sickening. The judge sat in his chair and watched as Daka condemned his mother.

The following mimics Daka's outburst, "This parent should not return home intact while I return to the eerie dungeon to await bullets at the public place. She had my soul, spirit, and body in her hands, but she showed no mercy as she squeezed hard enough without a pinch of compassion. Now my soul is done and gone. The spirit within me lays waste. And this body would be gone a little after dawn someday. The burly muscles will be no more because she imposed her will on me. I was this reliant, innocent, and defenseless child. I was ill-fated clay in my unimaginative molder's hands. She forced her uninspiring will on the naïve."

Brother KKK, I entreat that I am making an impression on you. You are my brother and my friend. I share my thoughts about life with you. What kind of parent are you? I knew you would ask what type of parent I am.

Do you impose your will on your children without looking at the larger picture? Do I force my way on my young ones without considering right and wrong? Do we compel our children to bear the burden of hate that we carried?

All parents have worlds of their own, but I admonish them not to pass anything that has no honor to their children. Children are bare lands to their parents. Some dump garbage on that beautiful piece of land. Some inundate it with filth. Others cultivate it with the best flowers available anywhere.

What do you do with your child, your own piece of land, Brother KKK? Do you load the land with piles of ego or bundles of humility? Some fertilize their lands with self-centeredness. Some enrich their own lands with charity. Do you nurture hatred on your piece of land? Or do you raise love on the land? Maybe you open the gate to your land and allow neighbors to dump dirt there. Reliable gardeners do not transform their gardens to public dumping yards. Responsible landscapers do not appreciate those who upturn trashcans on their lands. Unswerving parents neither edify malice nor hatred. They have no room for discrimination in their homes. They mold the most tolerant children parents could have.

Just like sheep depend on the shepherd in the field, children depend on their parents to determine which way to go in life. No matter what, valiant shepherds stand by their sheep. They scare away the wolves from surrounding bushes. Lions from the mountains cannot go near the sheep at night because the shepherds are not sleeping with their two eyes closed. In the same way, good parents guide and guard their children from learning evil. They cultivate hedges around their young ones, so the evils of this world would not creep into their midst. Honorable parents only teach their children honorable things. Regrettably, parents who do not know and do not know that they do not know teach their children dishonorable things.

Are you an informed or an uninformed parent? Informed parents appreciate that hatred has no reputation. They understand that prejudice has no place in a noble yard. I want to be a father on the alert. Neither malice nor bigotry would have a place in my home. I would not open my gates for wolves to sneak on my sheep. The vultures of this world understand they have no way of coming near my chicks. Teach your children good morals. Else, you will bear the burden of the evil that comes with the evil you tutored them. Admonish your offspring with love so they would bear the burden of the hatred they would generate if they did not listen to you. Be careful if you teach your children hatred. What if you reach the turning point some day and turn away from hate and your children have gone beyond redemption? Then you will bear the scar of the guilt you created forever.

Brother KKK, can you lend me your ears further? We have lived enough to start writing our own history. Man writes his own testimony every day. He tapes his own history with everything he says or does. The clever man only writes the best words in his testimony because every man has limited paper to write on. One cannot write and erase all he wants from the fragile paper of life. There is a limited eraser for erasing the bad words once you write them down. Our children are parts of our history. We cannot and must not write bad history for posterity. Valiant shepherds are gallant writers. They write the best of history for themselves. Their testimonies make the best reading anywhere. They write only what their children would not be ashamed of. They are not bothered by what posterity would read about them. They are aware that they are leaving good testimonies behind.

No matter what, wrong will only take the place of right at an unholy gathering. Hatred could partake in hate parades until eternity, but it would not displace love. Malevolent forces could try, but they would not attain the audacity to upstage the forces of good. Let hatred throw the dice forever. The face with dishonor will always turn up. Honor comes up when benevolence throws the dice just once. Why do parents teach their children hatred when evil forces, which hatred leads, cannot outshine benevolent forces? It is a colossal waste of time and monumental loss of energy for all who run against the wind to justify hatred as a better alternative to diplomacy. Running against flowing rivers cannot be as smooth as running with the water. Hatred means swimming against the current to reach honor when the latter waits downhill, but charity floats smoothly down the river to meet honor.

I can even prove that haters are enemies of the earth. Friends of the earth struggle to make the planet retain its greenness. They strategize to preserve the luxuriance and abundance of nature. They pursue the continuity of the diverse species with all of their might. Haters on the other side of the aisle seek to generate disaffection. Disaffection generates anger. Anger turns to conflict. Conflict leads to war. War creates destruction. The diverse species of living things are eliminated. Ecosystems are upset. Surroundings are poisoned with toxins from the deceased species. Man-made chemicals of mass destruction poison the environment. A multitude of species suffer for years, even centuries. Every man has two choices before him now. Man can be a hater and destroy nature. Else, he could be tolerant and love nature.

Let's teach our children love. They are agents of continuity for the diverse species of mankind. Love strives to tolerate, but hatred seeks to eliminate. Sowing disaffection among the coming generations of mankind is an unfair thing to do. Valiant shepherds do not create estrangement among their flocks. Good leaders carry all along without creating conditions that drift people apart. Generating hostility among children should not be one of the characteristics of a noble father. Heroic mothers do not create disaffection between kids. Great people do not nurture hostility among children. People with living faith sermonize love instead of hatred. The former comes from the Divine. The latter comes from a part of evil's agenda on earth. Real men do not hurt or kill on the basis of gangs. The art of sneaking up to slay or ganging up to eliminate people belongs to cowards.

Brother KKK, are you enjoying my missive of love? I think you should. This is an appealing advocacy. No one should be left out in the excitement of teaching our children tolerance. The time is right for fearless people to speak against the writing of hatred in the books that guide nations. Courageous men and women should reject those who legislate hatred in democracies. Spirited fathers and mothers should stand against judges whose verdicts separate children in schools on the basis of skin color. The faithful should be bold to speak against those who kill children in the name of God. Real associations must differentiate themselves from rabble-rousing mobs who seek attention in the wrong ways. Whoever is not excited by this advocacy needs a reality check.

What a people do with their children is a good yardstick for measuring decency in that society. The culture that raises loving and tolerant children is not deficient of honor. The people who raise prejudiced and extremist children have a dire future. Nobility would not find a place in the midst of the turmoil that the culture's children generate. In fact, you will lie in your bed just as you laid it. It is authentic when someone says you will garner whatever you sow. The people who guide their children well, just like good shepherds raise their sheep, would easily reap old age. Why? The children would bring honor to their families. Violence should be far from their hearts. The society that teaches hatred and malice to its children is in a different boat altogether.

The society that nurtures bigoted children who are willing to die so others might die would only reap grief in the end. What is left of a culture that raises its young so it could detonate them for some illusory agenda? What moral justification has the people who throw away diplomacy and embrace violence to make a point? Bloodshed has no place in the agenda of a loving and all-caring God. Murdering innocent people because of the policy of a government that hardly listens to its people's voice is not a fair game. Murder has a universal meaning. Unrepentant murderers would receive no mercy on Judgment Day.

The culture that grooms fraudulent youths because the elders stole and hid everything in foreign lands has nothing in common with accountability. The nation whose adults steal surreptitiously would only produce youth who steal clandestinely. Young people do not become armed robbers and marauders for no reason. Corruption is an endemic illness in a system that spools out corrupt youths as media prints press reels from newspapers. A society that makes its youths destitute in the presence of an unjustifiably wealthy, elitist clique has no business with morality. The decorousness of the youths produced by a society is truly a measure of its integrity. Deceitful youths usually take after corrupt adults as cubs take after tigers. The morality of the children raised by a culture is truly the product of that society.

What about a society that produces discourteous and unappreciative youths? When fate cuts a niche for young people, these youths rarely appreciate the nation and adults that give them so much. Parents mean little to them. Teachers deserve no thanks. They appear like acquaintances that should look the other way when young people are making their own rules. Public properties cringe in the presence of youths who vandalize. Illegal substances and strident carousing take over the streets at night. A society that raises impolite children cannot free itself from the mistakes of its youths. Young people are the products of societies that produce them. That is why the adults should take their own shares of the blame. Else, one would needlessly heave all of the blame on the youths. Young people seldom form their characters in a vacuum. A lot happens when adults look the other way more than necessary.

Brother KKK, I bet you now understand why I am advocating for valiant shepherds. The world needs thoughtful men and women who understand acceptance. They must be willing to teach tolerance to their children. These courageous guides should not be afraid of wrestling their young ones from the grip of hatred.

I pledge to be a noble shepherd. I will teach my children acceptance and respect for people who are different from them. Skin colors may be different, but all have similar red blood, bones, and marrows inside. I am aware that a black and white man could share the same blood type. A Christian and a Muslim could have the same type of marrow in their bones. A gang member's organ could work for the member of a rival gang, but the gangsters only generate a vicious circle of violence against one another.

I'm challenging you to a lovely mêlée, Brother KKK. Let's see who reaches the turning point first and sings the victor's song:

Great change since I saw the light
Great change since I saw the light
The things I used to do, I do them no more.
The hate words I used to say, I say them no more.

All the bad places I used to go, I go there no more.
The parades of hate I used to go, I go there no more.
There is a great change since I saw the light.

CHAPTER 13

▼

DÉJÀ VU

Violence never settles anything right. Apart from injuring your own soul, it injures the best cause. It lingers on long after the object of hate has disappeared from the scene to plague the lives of those who have employed it against their foes.
—Obafemi Awolowo

Brother KKK, what do you think when people turn their backs on diplomacy and form an alliance with violence? You would not agree with me more when you hear the story of the challenged state of Déjà Vu, the nation at war. Not only was she at war with her foes, she was at war with herself, too. Compared to the tens of her foes, hundreds of her people were dying needlessly on a daily basis. Regrettably, the war was lost. The battle was misplaced before the first volley of shots rang. No country had a better cause than Déjà Vu. There were good reasons for her to be angry. Her rationale for fighting would have been self-promoting. Good or bad, no one starts a fight without a reason, but there are good and bad ways of fighting.

She was a beautiful nation with a long phase of civilization. Déjà Vu, the beautiful, was the envy of friends and foes alike. Straddled by breathtaking landmarks and some of the most spectacular sceneries on the surface of earth, Déjà Vu was one of the untainted frontiers on the planet. From her soft, waving ocean to the sandy wilderness, the scenic highlands to the picturesque valleys, the incredible grasslands to the breathtaking oasis, Déjà Vu was truly a beauty to behold. The bonus for the beautiful nation's endowment was a stupendous gift of natural resources. Déjà Vu did not lack behind in term of human resources, too.

She had some of the most creative and dutiful people ever. Thus, a bully nation coveted her riches.

The intimidating nation was not satisfied with the cheap prices she paid for Déjà Vu's resources. She wanted more at cheaper prices. The bully nation resorted to blackmailing, arm-twisting, and cajoling, but Déjà Vu did not balk. Thus, the bully nation engaged naked force and started carting away Déjà Vu's possessions without paying anything ever again. The oppressive nation only bribed some of Déjà Vu's power brokers so they could stay silent. The repressive nation even offered to keep the bribe money in safe vaults in foreign lands, away from the prying eyes of Déjà Vu's people. Additionally, she started taking the best of Déjà Vu people as slaves. The real people of Déjà Vu revolted, but they understood that they could not match the offending nation's military on a one-on-one basis. Thus, they devised a plot whereby some of them would sneak into the bully nation's soil and wreak havoc.

These people from Déjà Vu were willing to die for their nation. They were eager to commit *seppuku* so their homeland's honor would return. The volunteers went to the bully nation and blended with the people. They staged a fake celebration and invited the orphans from that nation. The orphans were so grateful for the invitation because they were poor and always looking for their daily bread everywhere.

But the Déjà Vu suicide squad snared their guests. They laid a sprawling table of assorted food for them. The food's aroma was the most inviting thing for the pitiable orphans in a long time. Unfortunately, the Déjà Vu volunteers had poisoned the good-smelling food. They started eating and drinking the assorted dishes and juices first in order to convince their guests that it was appropriate to join the festivity. The Déjà Vu suicide squad and all of the orphans passed away shortly after the phony celebration began.

It was a painful day for the bully nation. No one was free from the sorrow that followed. The people of Déjà Vu, on the other hand, celebrated their horrendous feat in the streets. Regrettably, the rest of the world did not celebrate with them. Their friends, who believed in their cause originally, placed them at an arm's length after the atrocious exploit. Avoiding your foe's military and engaging violence against her defenseless people, including children, is a very good way to lose a war before it starts. It is a grand way to kill a grand cause. The nations that sympathized with Déjà Vu previously decided to stay out of what was to follow. They understood the injury that the nation of Déjà Vu inflicted on her people. She was a well-defined victim initially, but she turned herself into a monster nation that did not deserve any pity from the rest of the world.

The people of Déjà Vu trapped themselves. Every nation distanced itself from the unspeakable act of dishonor that its youths carried out. The nation that once had friends and sympathizers everywhere could barely find a single nation to relate to. Thus, it was a choking experience when it was payback time. It appeared like the bully nation was at liberty to continue with the rape of Déjà Vu without challenge. It now appeared legal for her to pillage the newly labeled "murderous nation of Déjà Vu." There was no good reason for other nations to face up to the pillaging of the challenged nation. She placed herself in that precarious position. The way one responds to an initial threat determines if people would stand by him or the threatening party.

The bully state did not terminate the acts of aggression. The nation of Déjà Vu did not back out. The chain of hostilities became longer. The vicious circle of violence did not unwind ever thereafter. Déjà Vu was clearly at the losing end of the spectrum. Overall, hundreds of her citizens were martyring themselves in return for a handful of victims falling in the other country. Every little loss inflicted on the bully state by Déjà Vu fueled the passion for revenge by the former. Every act of reprisal became more lethal than previous ones. Déjà Vu appeared like the unrestrained aggressor because she lacked the influence and resources to report the belligerence against her to the world. Meanwhile, the bully state had the might and resources to make the smallest act of aggression against her a huge headline around the world. It was an era of bad judgments for Déjà Vu policymakers. It was an epoch when everything went wrong.

Violence has never been an all-conquering weapon for fighting injustice. Its victory is short-lived. Its dark side overshadows its triumph. This is more so when the bullying party has an unrestrained capability to retaliate. More often than not, the oppressed party lacks the capacity to match the propaganda machinery of the oppressive party. People won the worst fights against injustice in the past without spilling an ounce of blood. If it was possible then, it is possible now. Clearly, Déjà Vu policymakers did not read about the travails of men and women who fought with the weapon called wisdom. After all, he who fights and runs away lives to fight another day. The warriors who know how to fight without the skill to retreat and regroup breathe their last before the time for winning the wars of their lives.

Déjà Vu leaders did not pay attention to the triumph of Mahatma Gandhi. Without throwing a rock, his peaceful philosophy injured the conscience of his nation's foes. Gandhi's famous nonviolent engagement influenced other peacemakers around the world. No scholar, wherever he resided in the world, was a real scholar without remembering Martin Luther King Jr. The 1964 Nobel Peace

Prize winner and icon of American civil rights movement drowned the clatter of hatred with the silent stroke of peace. He won the fight of his life without taking a pound of flesh. After his demise, he continues to live larger than life. Who passes the palace without revering the king?

Cesar Estrada Chavez, the civil rights activist and labor leader who led the struggle for better treatment of migrant workers in the United States, engaged the weapon called peace. He did not use either guns or bullets. Instead, he used a weapon that was potent enough to drill holes in people's hearts. Like raging water, a nonviolent crusade lacks hands, but it removes the mahoganies along its path.

Rosa Louise Parks was not certified to carry weapons, but she fought and conquered gun-wielding racists with the passive weapon called nonviolence. Her peaceful refusal to give up her seat led to the historical bus boycott in Montgomery, Alabama, in 1955. She did not have anything in common with sadism, but she won the fight of her life, too.

I admire the quest for peace of legendary Madiba Rolihlahla Nelson Mandela of South Africa. I do not think anyone on this planet has not heard about the famous prisoner, number 46664, of Robin Island, South Africa's most notorious apartheid penitentiary. The famous political prisoner did not subscribe to violence during his twenty-seven-year sojourn at the maximum-security prison. The penal colony, which was meant for hardened criminals, housed prisoners of conscience, but Madiba did not embrace aggression. Mandela, the conscience of Africa, shared the 1993 Nobel Peace Prize with former Prime Minister Frederik de Klerk for ending apartheid peacefully in a divided South Africa. Mandela became the first democratically elected president of South Africa from May 1994 to June 1999. Years after leaving power, Mandela did not stop talking peace from his Transkei hometown of Qunu.

Desmond Tutu, the 1984 Nobel Peace Prize winner, joined his nation's statesmen and engaged peace for resolving the problems that apartheid in South Africa generated. The archbishop and human rights activist did not make a pact with guns and ammunitions. Instead, he used guts and absolution. Kwame Nkrumah, father of modern Ghana and pan-African nationalist, set the agenda for the liberation of Africa. He did not allow the hangman's noose, which his nation's foes had woven, to find its way to his neck. He was a step ahead in the act of clean war. It is not clever to take a shower with gasoline when someone is waiting to set you ablaze.

Daw Aung San Suu Kyi, the Myanmar nonviolent prisoner of conscience and 1991 Nobel Peace Prize winner, knew how to down her foes without discharging a bullet.

Violence has no permanent victory. Naturally, it is a cruel form of a boomerang that turns around to hurt the body, soul, and spirit of the thrower. It starts by placing the nastiest label on its perpetrator. Then friends start getting suspicious of the violent person. Thereafter, foes and friends alike would have reasons to assume that the oppressed person was the problem. Hostility is a double-edged sword. If not well-directed, it cuts the foe or slices the sword-bearer himself. I am not aware of a lasting victory that comes out of violence. It could ward off the aggressor initially, but, at the minimum, it generates resentment in the long run. They say action and reaction are equal and opposite, but the backlash of violence is sometimes greater than the action it generates. Violence is not a panacea for warding off foes permanently.

Should the oppressed step aside and watch aggressors wreck their lives and those of their unborn children? No. The oppressed should fight every minute until their foes quit. However, there are good and bad ways of fighting. Nonviolence advocacy is the name of the weapon. It is cheap and pretty potent. People expect expensive medications to be more potent than the cheap ones, but that is far from the truth. Sometimes, the best things in life are not the expensive ones. Sustained nonviolence advocacy tickles the scruple of the oppressor. It rubs salt on the conscience, the open wounds on the hearts, of the conscientious members of the oppressive clan. Every land has its own share of conscientious men and women with senses of right and wrong. It is a matter of time. The foe's children would revolt against their oppressive fathers when the just cause of the oppressed batters their conscience.

I think I should illustrate the concept of nonviolence with another story. Once upon a time, when forest covered everywhere, nature created all animals to coexist happily without some imposing themselves on the rest. There was peace in the animal kingdom. All animals respected one another. The harmony that reigned once in the kingdom started diminishing with the advent of the lion's inordinate pride. Other animals respected him for his vigor and modishness, but the king of the jungle thought other animals did not deserve any respect from him. He was very rude and loud everywhere he went. He demonstrated his arrogance with his deafening roar, even when it was not necessary. Still, all animals revered him. The lion started taking the head chair at every occasion before they announced his name as the chairperson.

Bloated with pride, the lion started humiliating other animals. He found common grounds with other carnivorous animals. He convinced them to join him in making life miserable for other animals. The tiger, leopard, lynx, jaguar, caracal, and cheetah formed a class at the lion's behest. They made the jungle unbearable for the remaining animals. The lion became stubborn, and he ordered other animals to designate one of them as his meal every day. He ordered that the selected animal should stand at his door by sunrise. Otherwise, he would make the forest excruciating for all animals that day. Things degenerated to the level that many animals wanted to end the humiliation. Some were so furious that they went to his den to confront him. Unfortunately, the footprints of the animals that went to lion's den faced that direction. None of them faced outward. Obviously, the lion killed and ate all of them.

Boiling with anger, the giraffe went to the lion's den to face up to him.

"I'm the tallest animal in the jungle. Why should I stand and watch the lion treat other animals with disrespect?" he asked.

He ran to the lion's den, spewing anger from his nostrils, ears, and mouth. The lion heard his clattering hooves from far away and waited outside his den. Unfortunately, the giraffe's footprints headed toward the lion's den, but they did not head out ever again.

The deer went to confront the lion, but he did not return. The goat went after the deer so he could get his honor back, but he did not return, too. All of the animals' footprints went one direction without coming back. There was depression in the animal kingdom as more animals decided to die fighting instead of dying with humiliation.

The elephant and a few other large animals did not involve themselves in the clamor because the lion did not harass large animals. They had nobody to tell them that the strong men who watch marauders terrify neighbors without doing something are not strong enough. They lost their credibility to the lion for not raising a finger when the animal kingdom needed them. The large animals waited until the lion started harassing their young and weak ones before they started resisting. The lion misinterpreted the large animals' dormancy as weakness. He thought he could subject members of their families to the same treatment as other animals in the forest. The large animals now thought they should do something, but it was too late. Other animals no longer took them seriously.

Something strange happened at the least expected time. Tortoise, the little and slow animal who resided at the edge of the forest, had a bemusing suggestion.

"We've not been able to get our honor back because there has been too much anger and not enough wisdom. The fight is lost when it is fought with anger without acumen."

Many of the animals tried to shout the tortoise down. They could not relate what the slow animal said to the issue at hand.

"Who do you think you are? You are not Ojogbon Eranko, the knowledgeable and all-knowing animal," ridiculed the wolf.

The mocking wolf wagged his tail and howled at the moon as the meeting took place during the full moon. Other animals laughed and scorned the tortoise for his daring move. They accused him of rousing up a controversy so he could become famous.

"Someone is seeking fame here," suggested the sardonic wolf. "Aren't you seeking to be famous?"

The tortoise did not go into a noisy match with the derisive animals. He did not even try to explain himself because he knew nobody would listen to him.

Rather, the calculative animal surprised the other animals further.

"What would you say if I challenged the oppressive king of the jungle to a duel?" asked the diminutive animal.

The gathering burst into a ruckus as everyone became intoxicated with laughter. The jackal laughed until he became dehydrated because he lost so much water from his eyes.

"Well, I seek no popularity by trying to pitch in something at the critical moment in the lives of animals," clarified the undaunted tortoise. "It is not worth daring the merciless lion if fame is all you are seeking because you will die and lose everything anyway."

The other animals could not stop looking at tortoise astoundingly. The ants started entering the anteater's widely opened mouth as he gazed at the tortoise.

"Stop goofing. We don't kid around here. A serious meeting is going on," cautioned the ostrich.

The tortoise did not even respond to the ostrich's demeaning remark. He knew the latter as the tall fellow who buried his head in the sand and pretended that nobody saw him whenever a serious issue arrived.

"You don't even have brawny claws. How do you intend to fight the king of the jungle?" asked the ostrich, who would not keep quiet.

Still, the tortoise did not answer the mouthy ostrich. He knew how unwise it was to fight with a mouthy fellow in the dark. The tortoise understood that one could be pummeling the mouthy fellow, but he could be hailing himself as the one pounding the other person because it was dark and nobody could see the fight.

The tortoise understood that the lion planted informants among the animals. Thus, he sent an indirect message to the king of the jungle, challenging him to a fight at the town's square in three days. He gave some conditions under which he would fight with the lion. The tortoise requested that the lion should kill and eat him if he was conquered. Otherwise, all animals should get their freedom. The lion should not harass them again if the tortoise won. As expected, the lion's snitches informed him the following day. He was angry at first. The lion roared so thunderously that the whole forest was rattled. However, he understood the implications of not accepting the tortoise's challenge.

"A piece of cake," he remarked.

The lion asked his chef to think of a special recipe for cooking tortoise, assuring him that it would be dinner after his fight.

The end of the three days came so rapidly. The town square was agog with mischievous spectators who wanted to witness the lion eating the tortoise. The drummers hit the drums mercilessly. The singers went berserk as the animals held tree branches and danced themselves to a stupor.

"The tortoise rams into the king. He rams into the king. The king is not ached. He rams into the king. The slow fellow defies the king. He defies the king. The king is not defied. He defies the king. The tortoise dares the king. He dares the king. It's about dinnertime. Here's another free meal!"

All the animals watched the tortoise labor as he brought three gourds to his own side of the square. He was slippery with the paste of okra that he rubbed all over himself that evening. The animals did not applaud because they all expected to see the tortoise's downfall. There was an uncontrollable uproar as the lion emerged with all of his might.

"All hail the king!" shouted his yes-men.

His eyes were red like blood. His mane was ruffled like angry cobras. His tail was shooting like a furious arrow. All the animals along the lion's path moved backward as if the synchronization of ocean waves pushed them back. As usual, the lion's swollen head became even bigger. It was time for another animal that goaded the king to pay for daring the sovereign ruler of the jungle. But that was what the other animals thought.

The lion leaped forward and grabbed the little tortoise, but the latter slipped from his paws. The slimy okra paste that tortoise rubbed on his body was working already.

"It is neither by power nor might, but by wisdom," whispered tortoise, savoring his secret laughter alone.

The lion stormed forward and tried to grab the tortoise the second time. The slimy tortoise smiled as he slipped from the lion's paws the second time. There was silence everywhere in the forest as all animals watched the impossible becoming possible. How could the king of the forest miss a small and slow animal repeatedly? They could not believe their eyes. Maybe only the Divine was invincible. Some of the animals were about to reverse the earlier song in honor of the tortoise.

Incredibly frustrated, the lion jumped with all of his might, determined to pin the tortoise to the ground. Unexpectedly, the tortoise, the witty one, stepped aside. The lion landed on his own head and broke his neck. The tortoise carried one of the three gourds and smashed it on lion's side. The red solution inside spilled on the lion's body like blood. The smart animal carried the second gourd and broke it around the lion's nose. The material from it started dripping around the lion's nose, as if he were discharging mucous from his nostrils. The lion winced and started groaning as the pains around his neck progressed. Just then, the tortoise grabbed the third gourd and smashed it on lion's head. The gray matter inside smeared the latter's head, like his brain was coming out.

The shout of surprise was amazed and covered the jungle as animals ran from one end of the forest to the other, celebrating the fall of a cruel king. As far as the animals could see, the tortoise beat the lion until blood started coming out of his body. He tortured the king of the forest until mucous began to drain out of his nose. He also smashed the lion's head. Part of the king's brain came out. The shame was too much for the helpless lion to bear. He covered his face with his huge paws and groaned. His yes-men walked away from him as everyone departed him and his shame. The animals carried the tortoise on their shoulders and danced around the animal kingdom. The drummers hit their drums more than ever. The singers had the most entertaining day of their lives:

> Behold the new star in the sky
> Tortoise! A star was born today
> The fighting luminary of our time
> Tortoise! A star was born today
> One of its kinds in an era
> Tortoise! A star was born today
> What comes before fall?

Pride comes before downfall
Watch lion wincing wildly
Pride comes before fall
Watch arrogance groaning
Pride comes before fall

Brother KKK, can you see what I mean? Life goes beyond revulsion and aggression. There is more to life than violence. Wisdom solves the puzzle that sadism fails to decipher. Nonviolence means wisdom, as diplomacy equals astuteness. Stepping aside when the supercilious lion surges in your direction is wisdom. Presenting your case to the world tactfully shows how they wronged you. Killing to make a political statement blinds the world from seeing your point. If they fight wrongly, people lose their wars before they start them. The Divine is kind enough to provide conscientious allies for the oppressed among the citizens of oppressive lands. They rise against their nation's oppressive ways only when the oppressed do not put them off with violent behaviors. Every nation has its own share of conscientious people.

You could even make friends out of your enemies if making foes out of them does not improve your condition.

Abraham Lincoln said, "Am I not destroying my enemies when I make friends of them?"

Creating friends out of your antagonists could be a good way of combating them. But do not make friends of anyone who is cruel. Generating further enemies, in addition to your current enemies, by engaging in violent behaviors against defenseless people is a bad way of fighting one's enemies. Maybe policymakers everywhere should always remember, "Avoiding foe's military and killing defenseless people, including children, is a good way to lose war before it starts. It is a grand way to kill a grand cause."

People set their causes ablaze. They hardly rise from the ashes of condemnation after attacking defenseless children.

CHAPTER 14

▼

RISING PHOENIX

If we are to achieve a richer culture, rich in contrasting values, we must recognize the whole gamut of human potentialities, and so weave a less arbitrary social fabric, one in which each diverse human gift will find a fitting place.
—Margaret Meade

Brother KKK, you would pardon my desire for playing with words. Sip some patience water and enjoy the remaining episodes. I will bring the epistle to a close shortly. I am pleased that we are learning to be patient. Remember, we were not patient with one another years ago. Things have changed a little bit since the troubled years, but we have a lot of smoothing over to do. Have you ever marveled at the contrast between a colorful painting and a bland image done with a single color? The disparity between tolerant and prejudiced people is the same as the contrast between multicolored and plain images. Tolerant people see a colorful and diverse world, but prejudiced individuals see a routine and solitary planet where one way of life should thrive. The world is a coat of many colors.

What makes the world a beautiful place? The planet would have been a dull globe if it were made of a lone color. Thank goodness for the diverse colors that combined to make the world an enduring beauty with blue skies, azure oceans, gray mountains, green flora, brown earth, snow-white winter, dark night and stars, and diverse people, too! Who says diversity is not gorgeous? Tolerant people see fellow human beings in diverse colors, but prejudiced people see unusual people with whom they have nothing in common. Charitable people associate with fellow humans like they are brothers and sisters. Biased people relate to others only on the basis of the race, religion, association, or gang that connect them.

Broad-minded individuals create an endless world of freedom with unlimited horizons to explore. Prejudiced minds generate a severed world of anomy where fear and restrictions limit people's choices.

Diversity could as well be a synonym for democracy. Democracy was not a demon that was crazy. The Greeks were not crazy either when they gave the world the beautiful souvenir of democracy. My Greek friends say "democracy" emerged from two Greek words, "*demos*" and "*kratia*," meaning "people" and "rule." The independent city-states of Greece bequeathed the gift of government of the people by the people and for the people to the world. Thus, people with diverse skin colors, religions, associations, and opinions could seat at the table where the fates of nations are determined. They come with varied choices, but nobody walks away from the rest without returning to the table. I think that democracy is unity in diversity. Racists were, therefore, never democratic.

Mother Nature fashioned a beautiful world. Greece invented democracy so man could have egalitarianism. But man has yet to evolve from the state of social inequality. Nature equips all with diverse gifts, but focusing on selected gifts fascinates man more that harnessing the diverse gifts of all. Nature created nothing for which there was no use, except man has yet to discover the usefulness of all of nature's creations. I challenge someone to show me a man without a purpose. I would show him how little he understands nature. I dare somebody to show me a woman who does not know how to do something right. I would show him how faulty his observations were. Man sees the indolence in others when he is too lazy to see their admirable sides.

People see only what their inner eyes condition their outer eyes to see in other people. They do not see what they do not want to see, even when what they do not want to see stands directly in front of them and stares them in the face. He who has the mind and eyes to see the good sides of others sees diverse people with diverse gifts. Nonetheless, he who conditions his eyes to see something else sees superior and inferior people because other people's gifts are different from his. Mankind throws away the baby with the sullied water because he has yet to master the art of identifying and respecting diverse talents. Man loses the mainstream of talents from around the world when he celebrates only the laudable, but localized accomplishments that he trained his eyes to see.

These analogies sound familiar to me, Brother KKK. I saw it happening at my doorstep. You will probably agree with me after listening to the next story. Just twenty years ago, I was filled with praise and respect for responsible people. I learned early that responsibility was the quickest path to honor. It is no wonder that I had a lot of reservations for irresponsible people. I understood when someone worked so hard but couldn't make ends meet because of some reasons beyond his control. I also understood when someone had the opportunity to soar like an eagle but remained on the ground. Thus, I admired dependable people, but I was disappointed in reckless people. I assumed one had the choice to make himself either valuable or invaluable.

I drew my principle from the fact that I did a lot to pull myself up as a young person. I drew a line between resolute and irresolute people. I believed that everyone was the architect of his own fortune or misfortune in addition to destiny and luck. I held the unbending opinion that those who worked hard merited what they got. Those who messed up deserved what they had. Thus, I was not patient with indolent people. I was compassionate with those who deserved it, but I was rigid about rebuffing redemption for those who fell short.

"Whoever doesn't work should starve," I advocated.

Drunks and addicts were uncomfortable near me because I had no favor for them. And they knew it.

Somehow, fate offered me the chance to see the good side of an indolent, drunken addict who was a ne'er-do-well member of my community. The chance encounter provided me an opportunity to learn something new about people and circumstances. I found out that everyone had a purpose and nobody was useless. That was the day I questioned my opinion about rejecting redemption for ill-fated people. Everyone knew *Itu* as a skillful fighter. In fact "*itu*" means "feat" in Yoruba. The young man got the name because everybody thought he was good at fighting. He drank and abused drugs. He had no friends among responsible people, except people on the same boat as he was. I had no business whatsoever with him. But I would say "hello" grudgingly whenever he said that to me first. I thought there should be a permanent line between the troublesome member of my community and me.

Itu was a chauffeur. I needed to go downtown one day, but I could not find another vehicle. I had no option than to be in the car that Itu drove. Then something unusual happened. Sitting in the front passenger seat afforded me the opportunity to look outside the window as much as I wanted. Traffic was very slow. It even went to a standstill at some points. We were going through one of the idle segments of the journey when trouble came knocking. One of the newspaper vendors at the street corner held his paper to my face so I could see the headlines and patronize him afterward. I glanced at the headlines without touching the newspaper, but I did not see something captivating enough to grasp my attention. I looked away from the vendor and his newspapers, but that was not the end of the episode.

The vendor wanted me to buy a newspaper, regardless of whether I wanted it or not. I guessed he must have stood at the street corner for a long time without people buying newspapers from him.

"You have to buy the paper," he said, looking at me intently like he was seeking a fight.

I decided to avoid the man at first because I thought something was wrong with him. It was not unusual for vendors to display their papers in people's views when traffic slowed down. Not everyone who looked at the papers bought them. Clearly, the vendor was looking for a fight for no good reason. I thought he met the wrong person because I was not going to argue with him.

"Answer me, Mister. You have to pay for the paper for looking at it," he repeated passionately.

It was as if his existence depended on my purchase of the newspaper. I thought I understood his plight and would have bought one if he had behaved reasonably. However, I decided not to reward a bully salesman who rammed his goods into people's throats, regardless of whether they wanted it or not. The troublesome man started shoving the paper through the window and yelling.

"Give me the money for the paper now" he requested obsessively.

I wished the road could clear and vehicles should start moving again so I could avoid the tormenting vendor, but that was just a wish. That was when traffic decided to ground to a complete halt.

Apparently, I could not avoid the menacing fellow forever. So, I decided to act like a gentleman without caving.

"I'm the offended party here. You displayed your newspaper in my face against my will, thereby obstructing my view in a public place," I said, speaking like a legal practitioner.

I was not sure if I smiled or grimaced as I educated the man about how a good salesperson should conduct himself along a public road.

"I think everyone has the right to a clear view along a public passage without unwanted obstructions by fellow road users," I reasoned.

The desperate vendor would not have any of my scholastic arguments. He reached for my shirt's collar as the vehicle inched its way through the frantic traffic.

Then fate revealed to me that nobody was useless. Those who were written off could be useful sometimes. I was thinking about what to say next when help came from an unusual quarter. Itu got his name because he had the physique for accommodating trouble if he wanted. Muscular and six feet tall, he was a man who nobody would brush past without noticing. An elephant was not the kind of animal that someone would glance at without paying attention. Whoever saw an elephant had something to look at intently. Everyone around looked at the owner of the intrepid, deep, and unassailable voice when Itu spoke. I witnessed him saying something meaningful for the first time. I never expected something constructive from the troublemaker for once.

"Leave the gentleman alone. Don't make me come out of the vehicle," boomed Itu.

He did not expect any provocative verbal or bodily response from the newspaper vendor. I wished the muscular man could allow me to take care of the issue myself. I thought something appalling was lurking around when Itu gestured to finish the business on my behalf. I prepared myself to watch a big fight when there should not be any in the first place. The development gave me some goose bumps because I never liked violence. I was quick to speak against religious bigotry, inequality, and social injustices, but I hated violence in all of its ramifications. Just as nothing warranted avoidable aggression, nothing justified violence to me. One could make a point or generate a change without engaging in violent behaviors.

Brother KKK, I am glad to inform you that the expected violence did not have a chance. On seeing Itu's physique and scared face, the newspaper vendor walked away slowly. I could hear the unspoken words and soundless clapping from the hearts of the people around. Itu saved the day! Imagine the drunken addict who was a ne'er-do-well member of society playing the hero. I was as impressed as everyone around. The man who had been written off actually wrote off a sticky situation. Could it be that nobody was useless? Should there be redemption for those people who are written off? Is it unfair to give up on challenged people because of their circumstances? I started thinking quickly.

Maybe everyone is good at something if society would care enough to understand the good side of people instead of adopting condemnation before seeing through people. Maybe the world should offer redemption to challenged people instead of giving them judgment and prejudice. Suppose people should search for the good side of people instead of turning on the light and searching for errors in fellow humans. Nobody wants to inherit miserable challenges, but they come sometimes when one reserves no rooms for them. I challenge the world to extend goodwill to challenged people.

"I expect to pass through the world but once. Any good therefore that I can do or any kindness I can show to any creature, let me do it now. Let me not defer it for I shall not pass this way again," counseled Stephen Grellet.

Writing people off as well as disrespecting or judging others on the basis of race, religion, group, or association are not ideas that are thought out very well. Margaret Meade was right when she suggested a new world order that recognized all of mankind potentialities as an alternative to knitting a subjective social structure that disrespected other cultures and ways of life.

I join Margaret in requesting an inclusive world where the diverse gifts of the diverse peoples, faiths, and groups find fitting places. Then the world could boast of a tolerant civilization that is rich in complementing mores and values. It is not necessary to assemble a conglomerate of rocket scientists to fashion the new world order. Governments do not have to look far before finding the comprehensive social fabric.

Tolerance is the name of the new order that the component groups around the world need. Understanding is the nomenclature of the new bargain between the people around the globe. I squatted near my Muslim friend as the Imam joined him and his wife years ago. I was a Christian, as I am today, but I did not feel guilty for showing love to my friend in a mosque. The world seemed more beautiful to me when my friend sang out his heart in the church as the clergy joined my beautiful wife and me years later. My friend did not realize how I struggled to suppress tears from my eyes as he celebrated and smiled with me in a church building. That was tolerance. It was understanding and respect for one another's faith and way of life. We were the world.

Honoring my friend in a mosque did not harm my faith in any way. I guessed that my friend's belief was not impaired as he supported me in church. Didn't the two religions talk about unity, peace, and love? How do you demonstrate the three requirements of faith in a diverse world when you include some people and exclude others? Impulsive preachers should quit making enemies out of friends. Wasn't Abraham the patriarch of the faiths that his offspring founded? Agents of polarization should stop fracturing the world as they propagate their personal agenda. It is okay for Christians to have Muslim neighbors. It is fine for neighbors to partake in a barbeque sometimes. We are talking about a new social fabric for the world in order to avoid bequeathing a fractured world to our children. The new order should engender understanding from east to west as well as north to south.

Diversity enthralls me. In fact, television and newspaper advertisements with diverse people and ways of life appeal to me more than the rest. Why? That's how people like me see things. I am more comfortable and experience real unity, peace, and love when I attend a religious gathering with people of diverse colors. Why? Love is the name of my religion; tolerance is the nomenclature of my doctrine. I am bound by duty to send my children to schools where diversity thrives. Why? My children would live in a real world with the same people they would avoid if they attended segregated schools. The world is not a bubble anywhere.

Tolerance does not amount to turning your back on your race. It is about having an attitude of live and let live. It is not equal to giving away your culture. It is about going beyond lonesome traditions and enriching your world. You do not subjugate your faith by caring about the neighbor that professes a different religion. After all, the scriptures admonish faithful to love their neighbors as themselves. I do not recall the books encouraging believers to love some neighbors and exclude others. Tolerance announces your faith before you preach it. It demonstrates the power of love, forgiveness, and redemption possessed by your belief. Tolerance is far from giving away what makes you tough, but it saves you from the mental torture that afflict those who hate.

I am fascinated when reasonable cultural influences cut across one another. China and Japan have their differences with the United States, but Chinese and Japanese influences are all over the United States. There is no real American city without Chinese restaurants and Japanese martial arts. American cuisines and sodas are not strange to diners in many parts of the world. Tolerance opened the doors for Chinese restaurateurs and Japanese martial artists to own businesses in the United States. Tolerance encouraged Africans and Australians to accept American fast foods. Every land has its own catering, but diverse recipes from other nations open the door for choices.

Time is zooming by, Brother KKK. Let's rebuild this old house and find fitting places for all the stones. Building stones come in diverse shapes and sizes, but tested masons find fitting places for them all. Welcome to the new world, a magnificent house built with stones of dissimilar curves and dimensions. It is okay to disagree, but he who disagrees without agreeing would never be an agreeable person. Regardless of proximity, teeth and tongue disagree when the former inadvertently bites the latter, but they do not walk away from one another. Brides and grooms disagree, but Cupid does not stop shooting his charming arrows across the two hearts. Man should learn how to disagree without walking away from others.

Just as walking as a group creates confidence, working as a team heralds success. Just as a lonely group lacks the luxury of diverse experiences, the lonely man has no one to watch his back. The world is a book of many chapters and diverse themes. He who sticks to his race and does not venture out reads only a chapter. The group that shares nothing with other groups reads about a theme. The man, woman, or child who throws away others reads just one chapter. If the world is a book, educated folks who read a chapter are as ignorant as the illiterates who lack the ability to read. Who reviews a book brilliantly by reading a chapter? Is there a narrator who recites a book sufficiently by reading a chapter? I pity the illiterate for his inability to read, but I am disappointed in the learned who reads without comprehending.

Believe me, Brother KKK, he who strolls alone watches his back by himself. Whoever dares the storm of life alone suffers, no matter how strong. Traveling the road of life unaccompanied offers neither comfort nor security. Leveling the hills of life needs more hands than two. Filling the gorges of existence requires a lot of help. Your neighbor may lack the ability to bear the same quantity of filling material as you, but he is certainly throwing something into the frightening fissures on the ground. A gathering of hands gets a job done faster. Two hands lift and balance a bundle on the head better than one hand. Black, white, red, or brown, the world is crying for men, women, and children who are not afraid to work and walk with others to remake the world.

Crawling alone imperils the baby cobra. Who dare confronts a colony of snakes barehanded? A horde of cobras, diamondbacks, copperheads, cottonmouths, or coral snakes is not a pursuit for a marauding warthog. Show me the brawny man who would tackle a pack of ferocious carnivores at lunchtime. A squad of hungry lions, starving tigers, ravenous leopards, voracious jaguars, insatiable caracals, rapacious cheetahs, and famished lynx are formidable enough to scare the best of hunters. Agitated black widows, scorpions, stinging bees, hornets, and wasps are not playthings for a bored giant. No mountain is high enough to defy the valor of human potentialities. Additionally, no valley is low enough to breach the union of human strengths.

Imagine a community going it alone during an active and highly destructive hurricane season. How much of fun would he get? What if another community has no one to offer physical, emotional, and spiritual supports during a ravenous fire season? Picture the loss of a friendless people? Envision the plight of a disliked city founded where tempestuous tectonic plates meet? Earthquake victims could do with as many friends as possible when it hurts most. Remember the amount of support that came our way during the September 11 tragedy. Do you recall the outpouring of love and support from the world in the wake of the despicable acts of terrorism against our homeland? Our sorrow and anger would have gone through the top without someone somewhere somehow lifting a hand or raising his voice against the enemies of humanity.

No tribe is equipped enough to wade through the storms of life without friends. No race, people, or group is immune to vulnerability. We inhabit a dodgy world where vigilance is not enough. One hundred percent of alertness is a mirage in a world where the enemy needs one percent of success to make life bitter for others.

Imagine if one of the science-fiction moviemakers got it right and the aliens do invade our planet. What if they favor no race? What if they care less about religion? What if they do not give any consideration to groups or gangs? What if it takes the union of human possibilities, from the crudest to the most sophisticated, to turn the aliens back to their own planet? What if the invading aliens understand how to evade sophisticated weapons, but they are vulnerable to the crude ones?

Someone may argue how impossible this idea seems, but I am not talking about real aliens here. The challenges faced by mankind go beyond imaginary aliens.

Challenges began with creation, but mankind survived because they learned how to stick together. We subsisted because we knew how to weather storms together. Regrettably, man started creating obstacles along his way after tackling existing troubles. Like the fabled cricket that kept eating until its stomach burst, man keeps creating problems for himself until he is overwhelmed. Obviously, we have to understand that modern challenges are going out of the ordinary. We may not continue to be lucky unless we resuscitate the spirit of togetherness. We might not forever be a phoenix, the legendary bird that lived for centuries, set up a pyre in the wilderness, burned itself, and rose from its own ashes. We could become the rising phoenix that emerged from the ashes only if we remain together in the face of rising challenges.

More than ever, mankind needs to stick together as modern challenges become wilder to tame. Any race, people, or group that sets itself apart from others might learn the hard way that no culture, nation, or populace is immune to vulnerability. Modern challenges do not respect any power and might. It is now perilous for a people to rely on brawn because the enemy understands how to use people's power against them. Worse still, any race, people, or group that finds common ground with violence would go down under the weight of a united world. We cannot and must not sever the chord of brotherhood that tied mankind together in the beginning. The United Nations should be about unity, peace, and love, not power, politics, and bickering.

You and I have a lot to do together, Brother KKK. It is time to rebuild the broken bridges that link all of human races. Let's bridge the tempestuous oceans that separate mankind into feuding brothers. We have to remove the thorns that cover the paths that connect our communities. Let us be the generation that averts a polarized world for the coming generations. We are the final glowing chunks of coal in a weary world. Let's stop dumping each other in wet places. We are the bastions of hope in a worn earth. Let's rebuild a beautiful world. Let's fortify our children as the reinforcing cement in a fractured world. We must stop brothers from engaging in a senseless war of attrition.

Brother KKK, the world is growing older, but she is not acquiring wisdom as she amasses prejudice. Wisdom means creating a way where there seems to be no way. Wisdom equals squeezing peaceful water out of the stone of hatred. Wisdom amounts to bringing out the beauty that lives in ugly. There is wisdom when all races coexist happily without some using arbitrary yardsticks for measuring human potentials while minimizing the potency of the potentials that others possess. Wisdom means finding fitting places for all human stones in the magnificent building called the world. Wisdom amounts to all working together and building a friendly world for the coming generations of mankind. There is wisdom when we bring down the curtains of prejudice, fanaticism, and self-destruction that separate us.

CHAPTER 15

▼

IRON CURTAINS

The time is always right to do right.
—Nelson Mandela

Brother KKK, I told you this letter would soon come to an end. Whatever has a beginning has an end. You and I will come to the end of our sojourn on earth someday. We can depart as heroes who identified good causes and stood by them, or we can be tyrants who learned evil and held onto it naïvely. Whichever way we choose to exit the stage of life, consequences exist. Every man writes his own testimonial every day of his life. Your testimonial will determine if many generations will celebrate your life when you are done and gone. Mine will decide if posterity will be proud of me. We are the architects of our legacies and the designers of the epitaphs on our tombstones. Martin Luther King Jr. and Adolf Hitler must have figured that out by now.

As youths, we held onto pride tenaciously. Wisdom demands that we take strides toward nobility now that we are old and spent. Take a moment to think about your exit and what the world will think about you thereafter. It seems like yesterday when we were tots. Still, years from now would remain like yesterday when we become old and weary. Think about your demise whenever you witness a peer's funeral and reflect over what your grandson's peers would say about his grandfather. Soon, pride would go into the grave with its arrogant owner, but benevolence would tarry and celebrate the life of its charitable owner. In the end, all who fought and died over land would realize, to their chagrin, that all they really needed was a six-by-four plot of land—the grave.

I send all of my adoration to everyone who refuses to be a part of the problem and becomes a part of the solution. My heart goes to every man who lifts a hand to make the world a better place. I doff my hat for every woman who speaks against prejudice. I salute every child who refuses to imbibe the wine of hatred. I offer nothing but tribute to real preachers who preach tolerance in place of hatred. Ever will the members of the clergy who offer grace to all nations earn my respect. You are the wind beneath the wings of a weary world. All hail the giver of the kiss of life without which the world would choke on its own antics. I celebrate the lives of the fallen as well as the innocent and defenseless victims of hate crimes around the world.

Brother KKK, are you with me? It is time to identify all who plan to bequeath a peaceful world to their offspring. The time has never been better for mankind to know who is on the side of harmony. All who truly love their children should raise their hands and let the counting begin. It is sweet at this time to isolate those who wish a peaceful life for their children but fan the amber of hatred. The world deserves to know those who sabotage the universal brotherhood of man. Our children cannot continue to lose the freedom to please their curiosity because they cannot explore some regions. Let's break down the stockades of narrow-mindedness. Parapets of hate shall fall. Groups will no longer detest other groups. Tear down the barricades of gangs that obstruct brothers from seeing eye to eye.

Let's rip down the walls of racism, the fence of religious bigotry, and the barriers of inequality. Let's smash down the walls of polarization and shatter the fence of severance. Let's fracture the barriers of radicalism and rupture the walls of chauvinism. Grant mankind the wisdom to quit playing into the hands of agents of polarization who engage what is dear to man—that is, race, faith, and association—to divide mankind. Let our children entertain no fear when traversing neighborhoods where different cultures live. They should have no cause to fear when passing the homesteads of those who embrace different religions. Let's take all neighborhoods back from treacherous gangs. Let there be trust among nations and peace between faiths. Let man be civilized enough to appreciate diversity.

Peace, have your way. Harmony, fill all nations. Unity, take over the world. Concord, find your feet in all lands and climes. Let friendship abound in the world. Let camaraderie become a native of all countries. Let all youths who naïvely plan to sacrifice their souls think before accepting martyrdom for the agenda they knew nothing about. Why do youths fail to question why those who request them to sacrifice their bodies fail to surrender themselves, their children, or members of their families for the same cause they wanted other people's children to commit suicide? Why are the merchants of death not sending their own children to heaven if painful death is the only path to heaven? Why do they run when death beckons at them?

"Be wary of the man that urges an action he himself incurs no risk," said Joaquin Setanti.

The fact that many followers allow others to make their minds up for them explains why people accept death, hook, line, and sinker without asking questions before committing suicide.

Now I understand why Hitler said, "What luck for rulers that men do not think."

I admonish followers to choose between believing in God or the preachers who substitute their own agenda for God's. The follower who kills at the order of a preacher is not obeying God when the all-caring, all-loving, and all-forgiving God orders man not to kill. It is not logical to assume that the all-knowing God, who knows the future, would do a rethink and order man to kill after commanding him not to kill. Besides, the all-powerful God does not need a man to kill on his behalf when miraculous things happen at the sound of his voice. He has the power to take lives as he wants without man's input.

Let there be tolerance from Ankara to Brussels as well as Copenhagen to Dublin. Altruism must rear its beautiful head once again in Abuja, Bogotá, Cairo, and Delhi must turn over a new leaf. Washington DC must tell Ottawa, London, Berlin, and Paris that the long journey to civilization is a waste of time without the peaceful coexistence of mankind. Moscow, Beijing, Pyongyang, and Havana have roles to play in remaking the world. Riyadh should tell Kabul, Islamabad, Tehran, and Damascus that diplomacy is the answer. Unity should be the centerpiece of Canberra, Tokyo, Oslo, Stockholm, and Vienna's foreign policies. Accra, Algiers, Abu Dhabi, Brasilia, Buenos Aires, Budapest, and Port of Spain should be anchors of harmony.

Allow justice to flow from north to south. Let impartiality stream from west to east. Permit Jews to have a reunion with their Arab brothers. Give Abraham the chance to rest in the grave. Let forgiveness run from Africa to America as well as from the Middle East to Europe. Blacks and whites should widen their horizons and embrace the human race instead of limiting themselves to black and white comfort zones. Red or brown, skin color resides only on the outside. Red blood runs through all of us. Let man respect and elevate himself from the level of the dog that eats dog. What use is knowledge if people do not treat one another better than the animals in the wild? Why does man change knowledge from beautiful to ugly by engaging knowledge for destructive acts? Let the bird that lives at home inform the one that resides in the bush that a new world order must surface.

Mankind needs a few conscientious men and women to protect him from himself. Time is zooming by, but "better late than never," they say.

Let us arise, Brother KKK, and rebuild the world. Our children are teetering on the rim of the treacherous cliff that the generations before us made. This present generation has perfected this cliff. The endangered world needs you and me, Brother KKK. Never grow weary or doubt your ability to change the world because you are an individual. You could change the world by teaching tolerance to one child at a time.

"To the world, you might be one person. But, to one person, you just might be the world," advised a sage.

Do not allow the weariness of being an individual who could not change the world all by yourself overwhelm you. There is power in individuality when it has something for all. Electricity was one person's idea, but it changed the way the world does things. The telephone was an individual's initiative, but it changed the way that the world communicates. You and I could talk to one child at a time about getting along with others.

A daily rendition of freedom song without stopping parades of hate should be out of the question. Permitting hateful citizens to humiliate law-abiding citizens is the peak of irresponsibility on the part of any government that sings about freedom for all. Whoever assumes that hateful parade is an expression of freedom must be living hateful life, intentionally or unintentionally. Today, bigots parade the streets, expressing hatred for others. The government watches without lifting a hand.

"Freedom of speech and expression," they explain.

What if assassins, armed robbers, pedophiles, and fraudsters take to the streets tomorrow and ask for their own freedom of speech and expression?

Thank goodness for freedom. But responsibility comes with freedom. Freedom that hurts some people should not be absolute in a responsible society. It is irresponsible to hide behind freedom of speech and say or do hurtful things to others. Life expects much from whomever it offers much. We should not abuse freedom by engaging in parades of hate. The nation that grants some citizens the freedom to flaunt hatred in the streets in the guise of freedom of speech and expression lacks the audacity to grant freedom to all of her citizens. Like all good things of life, including food, water, and air, inordinate freedom hurts when abused. My freedom ends where yours begins. Yours ends where mine starts. Let's start talking to families, friends, and neighbors about tolerance. Our children should not lack the freedom to get along with other children simply because they belonged to other races, religions, or cultures.

The first step in staying away from intolerance is to stop associating with those who hate others. The sheep that hangs out with the dog starts eating what the dog eats soon. It is easy to say that you will not do what your friends do, but it is not easy to distance yourself from what they do or say. People are tempted when they associate with a hateful crowd.

They say, "If you show me your friend, I'll tell you who you are."

Do not listen to haters or partake in their talks. Involuntarily, just like the body mimics nature, humans mimic what they hear. Remember, you feel like urinating when you hear water running. Thus, people have reasons to despise others when they listen to those who do not see anything good in others. I advise children to look for role models elsewhere if their parents hate. Many baby sharks flee from bad mothers after birth so the latter will not eat the former.

Those who make coffins may not be happy as the rest of the world prays for longevity, but all who care about good health should not stop praying. Racists, terrorists, and gangsters may not be happy with agents of unity, but those who build bridges between cultures should continue. Keep the ideals alive even when all remains risky. Time will tell who was telling the truth. Remember Galileo Galilei, the renowned Italian astronomer, philosopher, physicist, and mathematician? He was harassed, arrested, and incarcerated for telling an all-time truth that the sun was stationary and the earth (among others) revolved around it. If they were around, all who persecuted the great astronomer would agree on one thing today. Politics changes, but the truth remains constant.

As a young college graduate, I was frustrated more than two decades ago because I could not satisfy everyone around me. I sometimes had different opinions from some people, but I wanted to be on the same page with everyone. I found out that, the more I tried, I could not satisfy everyone. I discovered the secret of silent laughter the day I realized that I should not give up honorable opinions, dreams, and beliefs because everyone did not agree with my ideas. I recalled that everyone who witnessed the deeds of the founders of the popular religions did not agree with them anyway.

"Who am I to assume that everyone would agree with me?" I reminded myself.

These days, I ask myself, "How would the Divine react to an issue? What does my conscience say?"

The two now work together. The Divine speaks with me through that little voice inside of me to make me do his will. Thereafter, I stand by whatever the silent voice identifies to be honorable. Then I hold on firmly to the honorable choice, even as the storm of life rages. You may not be able to change everyone around you, but you should never give up the ideal of leaving the world better than you met it. Change one child at a time. Stop the world from slipping into chaos. There is no end to doing what is honorable until the day you die. This is my advice to all who believe in rebuilding the world.

"All receive advice; only the wise profits from it," counseled Publilius Syrus, the Roman epigraphist.

Forget about politics. All with a conscience should raise their hands and let the counting begin. Welcome to the big task, United Nations secretary-general. Intolerance is an alarming reality of our time. Undoubtedly, you are chipping in something, trying to rebuild the world. The Pope should not hesitate to speak peace with the grand imam of Mecca. We all dwell in one world with one destiny. We could only loathe one another to the peril of mankind. It is okay for the king of Saudi Arabia to speak with the venerated Archbishop of Canterbury. One does not become a smoker by smoking a peace pipe. Religious bigotry apart, no one loses his faith by loving others. God was God because he was loving, peaceful, caring, forgiving, understanding, and not petty like humans.

The president of the United States of America and that of Russia would achieve more if the pursuit of happiness for all of mankind were their primary agenda. Unhealthy rivalry should have no place in their lexicon. Time is running out, prime minister of the United Kingdom, German chancellor, presidents of France and Italy. Accept the opportunity to become world statesmen and women of the new era. Do not limit your horizons to your realms. Nations that dump toxic waste on others should remember that what goes around comes around. The era of offering one bag of aid to the poor and carting away ten bags from them should end. The world looks up to you, emperor of Japan, prime ministers of Canada, Australia, and Belgium. Please save man from himself.

You bear the destinies of many generations in your hands presidents of Nigeria, South Africa, Côte d'Ivoire, and Uganda. People should not be thirsty when there is water everywhere. Not only will you account for what you did, you will also account for all that you failed to do. The king of the land of spirits would audit your commissions and omissions someday. Answer the call to duty leaders of the Central African Republic and Mali. Presidents of Chad and Burkina Faso should pay attention to the clarion call. There is more to leading than dwelling in palaces that are fenced away from the people. Whether you sleep in bed or on a mat, day will break at the same time. Buried in gold caskets or ragged shrouds, we will all become nourishment for the soil some day.

Let's remake the world leaders of Brazil, Argentina, Mexico, and Colombia. President of Afghanistan should request the Syrian leader to accompany him to Iran. He should stop by at the palace of Saudi Arabian king and invite his royal highness. He should call the prime minister of Lebanon and president of Palestine to go with him. Then, he should tell all nations that have good causes to present their cases to the world peacefully. Violence is a grand way to kill a grand cause. Presidents of Egypt, Ghana, Libya, and Liberia, liberate the cradle of civilization from poverty.

Advocate for human rights for all of humankind, presidents of China and Cuba. Prime minister of South Korea and chairman of North Korea can generate progress for their nations if they work together. Unwholesome rivalry cannot take the place of constructive competition. Prime minister of India and president of Pakistan would end the war of attrition at the frontiers if they would work together and usher advancement into Southeast Asia. Help bring harmony back to the world, prime ministers of Slovakia, Papua New Guinea, and Bhutan. President of Uruguay and king of Bahrain can add voices to peace talk around the world. Stop the hardships, presidents of Zimbabwe, Sudan, Rwanda, Congo, and Somalia.

Brother KKK, I sense that all may not agree with me, but we could make the world a better place. Like a swift river, we could make justice flow from high to low places. Let's entreat tolerance to cover the world as water covers the sea. Like fire ravages the wilderness, implore the Divine to permit charity to sweep across our planet. Let fairness soak the earth like rain waters the tropics. May the spirit of patience that transcends fanaticism take over the world. Never again shall man descend into a chasm and haunt fellow men like animals in the wild. Let the merchants of death do a rethink. Ela, the peaceful one, climb down on our world. Man is self-destructing, and tranquility is fading. Climb down, Ela, the judicious knight.

Tear down the iron curtains of hatred, prejudice, religious bigotry, and gangs that fracture the world into belligerent factions. Rip down the rigid curtain of intolerance that separates races, religions, and cultures, the curtain of discrimination that brings man to the level of dogs that eat dogs. Gash the curtain of oppression that makes nations subjugate nations politically, economically, and culturally.

Let there be love at homes. Let there be cheerful faces on the streets. May there be tolerance and patience in the morning, afternoon, and evening. Let love rule our children's day and broad-mindedness govern their night.

He who must be a racist should join me and become a special racist. I finally figured out how to be a racist without getting into trouble. I am passionate about my race, and I am proud to be a racialist. Which race do I belong to? That would be the human race. My race boasts of diverse members. There are whites, blacks, and other people of color. We have Africans, Americans, Asians, Australians, Europeans, Caribbeans, Middle Easterners, Pacific Islanders, and others. We are all passionate about the human race, and we are proud to be. Please, join our race. Universal brotherhood of man is our agenda. We are the cement that bolsters the fractured world. Our members build bridges among peoples and nurture understanding among cultures.

We have honorable men and respectable women in the race. We even have children whom we have raised to love there. Our race is about the contents of people's characters, not skin colors. It is about what we do with our faiths, not religion. It is about the amount of love that is rooted in our hearts. We care about humanity, not nationalities. Class has no place in our race, but humility does. We care about accountability, not bank accounts. Our race is one large gang of diverse people who claim memberships of the human race. We are color-blind. Peace is the only sign that we throw around. Harmony and love are the only weapons we carry.

Imagine being a member of a race where Christians have Muslim neighbors and their children have no reasons to dissociate from each other. Visualize being a part of a group where people wish people well, regardless of the languages used for that purpose. Picture the joy in the assembly of men, women, and children that treat all and sundry with respect. "People" is the name of our religion. Humanity is the bottom line of our agenda. We understand how restrictive it is to limit oneself to a race. The whole wide world is our constituency. Are you still wondering why you should be a racist like us? Join the human race if you must be a racist. This is the only race you could possibly claim without getting into trouble with the court of public opinion. Please join the human race and lose nothing except prejudice.

Where is your sting, hater? Soon, you will depart unsung. Comets shall not dazzle the skies at your demise, and man will not celebrate your life. There shall be no requiem for you. The day shall not smile for you. Night shall not yield stars to watch your footsteps as you tread the somber path of damnation. Men shall remember when you dug a hole in the ground, covered it with mats, and tricked defenseless people into walking across. Women shall recall that you wore a garment of thorns when fellow humans tried to lean on you. Children will commit to memory how you packed your mouth with ground pepper when they requested you to blow dust out from their eyes. The world shall call to mind how animosity clouded your judgments and prejudiced your rulings.

You have it coming, religious extremist who kills in the name of God. You are the coward who murders commonplace men, defenseless women, innocent children, and frail elderly. You will not know what hits you when the Divine denies you at the last moment. You misrepresent God and interpret the scriptures to suit your ill-fated agenda. How dare you jettison the verses that talk about unity, peace, and love and literally pursue the parts that dwell on fatality? Who can say for sure that the verses are not parables, meant for bringing contrast to the scriptures? Maybe God's thought is far from death where the books talk about death. What will you do if you find out that God's thought is far from man's agenda more than Mercury is farther from Neptune? Think, think, and think again!

To all who hate, I counsel you to cease from detesting fellow men. The world may not understand your standing. The members of your group may never celebrate you as heroes. Hatred is no longer fashionable. People no longer boast about prejudice without getting into trouble. I tell you that it is not too late to reach the turning point. Stop the irritating velvet beans in you from growing. Nobody harvested the ones that fruited previously; the itchy hairs on the beans deterred people from harvesting them. The world would crave your beans if they stop producing itchy hairs and begin to offer nutrients to the people. The hater who turns a new leaf and speaks up for tolerance would become a real hero.

No one puts on the light and hides it. Man displays all things that make him proud. Whatever man does in the dark, it is nothing to be proud of. People with integrity come clean as they have nothing to hide. Dishonest people transact businesses in the dark. Honorable associations meet in the open. Their agenda is nothing except goodwill for all. On the contrary, dishonorable associations meet behind closed doors. Their schema thrives on secrecy. Any association that has its agenda rooted in illegal substances is yet to share a common ground with honor. The coalition that has nothing in common with hunting, but brandishes deadly weapons, has nothing to offer the community it is situated. I beseech our youths to call it quits with gangs for their own good.

Brother KKK, just as I wish mine would earn me, I wish your testimonial would earn you the following words when you take the final bow on the stage of life:

> Done and gone, but his spirit lives and gives. It gives strength to those who rebuild the world so the coming generations of mankind would live in peace.

Humanity was the name of his race. Love was his religion. Tolerance was his agenda.

Please join me in entreating tolerance to take the place of intolerance in the hearts of our children and have charity take the place of prejudice. May unity illuminate our youths' day, peace brightens their noon, and love lights up their night. This far, I guarantee my love for you and your family. My neighborhood remains free for you. My abode is a safe haven for your children.

Thank you for your patience. The letter is coming to an end, but this is the beginning of what we could do together. We have the destinies of generations of mankind in our hands. Together, we could end the petty, immature, and unhealthy squabbling among races, faiths, and groups. We could do a better job of making the beautiful world even more beautiful. Please feel free to take the message herein to a new level. Discuss the contents with your family, friends, neighbors, colleagues, acquaintances, or whoever cares to listen to you. Challenge everyone you know to read the letter. Let me reemphasize that our generation would have failed cheerlessly and we would have fallen short as individuals if our wounded today would become our children's unhealed tomorrow when we are done and gone. We could only ignore or treat intolerance as the norm to the peril of our children and the generations after them. I wish you all that I wished myself.

Regards from a brother, who cares,

Dele.

978-0-595-47082-2
0-595-47082-3